AF600496

Delinquencies and Penalties in the Administration and Reception of the Sacraments

A DISSERTATION

Submitted to the Faculty of Sacred Sciences of the Catholic University of America in partial fulfilment of the requirements for the Degree of

DOCTOR OF CANON LAW

by the

REV. GEORGE LAWRENCE MURPHY, J.C.L.
of the Archdiocese of Philadelphia

1923

Nihil Obstat.

†THOMAS J. SHAHAN,

Censor Deputatus.

Washingtonii, D. C., die XXIII Aprilis, 1923.

Imprimatur.

†MICHAEL J. CURLEY,

Archiepiscopus Baltimorensis.

Baltimorae, die XXIII Aprilis, 1923.

CONTENTS

INTRODUCTION

The Church, bearing in mind the warning words of her divine founder, "Give not that which is holy to dogs; neither cast ye your pearls before swine,"[1] has always zealously safeguarded the sacraments from abuse. In the very beginning of Christianity, for example, St. Paul sternly reprehended some of the Corinthians who profaned the Lord's Supper by their riotous feasting, thus rendering themselves unworthy to receive the Eucharistic Food.

After the persecutions abuses in the administration and reception of the sacraments became more frequent. Hence it was found necessary to resort to punitive measures. Penalties were enacted against the practice of rebaptizing heretics on their entrance into the Church, against the crime of simony, especially as it manifested itself in the sacrament of Orders, and also against other offences that not only dishonored the sacraments but also threatened to bring them into disrepute.

Thus a number of penalties grew up for maladministration and illicit reception of the sacraments. But before the Code there were still many cases for which no specific legislation had been enacted. Some penalties, too, that had been embodied in *the Corpus Juris Canonici,* because they were not renewed in the constitution "*Apostolicae Sedis*" of Pius IX, automatically ceased to exist. For instance, this happened to the *latae sententiae* penalties decreed against the crime of simony.

The New Code, however, seems to have covered the ground pretty thoroughly. Some penalties have

---

1 Matthew 7-6.

been taken over bodily from the Old Law, others, which had passed out of existence, have been revived, and also several new punishments have been introduced. The most important of these new punishments is found in canon 2364 which provides a penalty for all cases in which the sacraments are administered to those prohibited by divine or ecclesiastical law from receiving them. This canon is contained in the sixteenth title of the fifth book of the New Code, in which also are comprised eleven other canons dealing with the various individual sacraments with the exception of the Holy Eucharist and Extreme Unction. While these two latter sacraments are not separately treated, nevertheless offences committed in administering them to those to whom their reception is forbidden is punishable by canon 2364, and so it can be said that now penalties exist for abuses connected with all the sacraments.

In the present dissertion we discuss these canons. The more important canons, of course, receive greater consideration than those of less practical import, but all are treated as fully as the necessities of a clear interpretation demand.

CHAPTER I

THE SACRAMENTS IN GENERAL

Prior to the New Code penalties had been decreed at various times for the offence of administering the sacraments to certain classes of unworthy or unqualified recipients. For instance, in the decretals of Gregory IX (A. D. 1234) we read that all heretics incurred an excommunication, and that clerics must not give them the sacraments. For a violation of this law clerics should be deprived of office. To recover the office a special indult of the Apostolic See was necessary. Regulars, too, might suffer the same penalty, and in addition forfeit any privileges they enjoyed in the diocese in which the crime was committed.[1] Similarly, Boniface VIII (A. D. 1298) legislated that if a cleric should administer the sacraments to an excommunicated or publicly interdicted person, he was to be forbidden ingress to the Church until he had rendered sufficient satisfaction for the offence.[2] There were penalties also against the practice of rebaptizing persons already washed by the laver of regeneration. Both the minister of the sacrament and the person rebaptized contracted an irregularity. Moreover, clerics were to be deposed and lay persons excommunicated.[3]

But there was no general legislation covering the illicit or invalid administration of the sacraments to all classes of persons disqualified by divine or ecclesiastical law from receiving them. This defect is now remedied. Canon 2364 declares that a minister who presumes to dispense the sacraments to those who by divine or ecclesiastical law are forbidden to

1 C 13 X de Haereticis V 7.
2 C 8 de Privilegiis V 7 in Sexto.
3 Schmalzgrueber P. 1 Title IX N. 36.

receive them is to be suspended from administering the sacraments for a period of time to be determined by the prudent judgment of the Ordinary; he is to be punished also in other ways according to the gravity of the offence. Besides, other particular punishments ordained by law for delinquencies of this kind retain their penal force.

Hence, by virtue of this canon, all offences which consist in the administration of the sacraments to those to whom their reception is forbidden by law, most of which were not canonical crimes in the Old Law, are true crimes, that is, external and morally imputable violations of the law to which canonical sanctions are attached. From this we see what wide penal powers are now vested in the Ordinary in this connection.

A list of the delinquencies punishable by this canon must be drawn from those canons which inhibit the use of the sacraments or prohibit their dispensation absolutely or under specified conditions to certain individuals. Accordingly, violations of the following canons will constitute the crimes embraced in the scope of canon 2364. Those canons, however, for whose non-observance a special penalty is provided, as, for example, in canon 2367, will not be included in the list which follows.

(1) Persons who are not members of the Church through the sacrament of baptism are incapable of receiving the other sacraments.[4]

(2) Those who are excommunicated or personally interdicted are forbidden to receive the sacraments.[5] In danger of death absolution from these censures can be given by any priest, even though he should not be approved for hearing confessions, and after the absolution, if the person be properly disposed, the last

4 Canons 786, 853, 901, 940, 968, 1012.
5 Canon 2260, 2275.

sacraments can be administered.[6] In case the censure were reserved *ab homine* or *specialissimo modo* to the Apostolic See, the penitent, on recovery, would have to make recourse in accordance with the provisions of canon 2252.

Administration of the Sacraments to Heretics and Schismatics

(3) It is forbidden to administer the sacraments of the Church to heretics or schismatics, even though they be in good faith and request them, unless, having adjured their errors, they become reconciled to the Church.[7]

This canon has given rise to considerable discussion among canonists and moral theologians, especially in regard to the matter of administering the sacraments of penance and extreme unction to an unconscious or dying heretic or schismatic. The common opinion gives it a rather liberal interpretation. Pruemmer, for example, states "Iste canon videtur esse illimitate applicandus haereticis et schismaticis bene valentibus; qui, tamen, si sint moribundi et bene dispositi possunt privatim absolvi a censuris et peccatis, etiamsi propter defectus temporis aliaque impedimenta gravia prius nequeant induci ad explicite rejiciendos errores et ad reconciliationem Ecclesiae."[8] Vermeersch expresses practically the same opinion: "Excipiendum est periculum mortis, in quo modis omnibus qui in theologia morali explicantur, illos quantum copia nobis est juvare possumus ac debemus."[9]

The predominant idea seems to be to do all that is possible for the eternal salvation of a dying heretic or schismatic without, however, subjecting the sacra-

6 Canon 882.
7 Canon 731, par. 2.
8 Brevis Conspectus Mutationum Theol. Mor. p. 5.
9 Summa Novi Juris Canonici, N. 278.

ments to the danger of irreverence. This attitude is supported and confirmed by the following response of the Holy Office, May 26, 1916:

An schismaticis in mortis articulo sensibus destitutis absolutio et extrema unctio conferri potest? Resp. "Sub conditione (cum de intentione aliisque in poenitentia ad valorem requisitis dubitari debeat) affirmative, presertim si ex adjunctis conjicere liceat, eos implicite saltem errores suos rejicere, remoto tamen scandalo, manifestando scilicet adstantibus (qui id nesciant) Ecclesiam supponere eos in ultimo momento ad unitatem rediisse." [10]

Some canonists think that probably conditional absolution may be imparted to a formal and public heretic or schismatic deprived of his senses.[11] This opinion is not in clear conflict with the decree just quoted, at least in respect to schismatics. On the contrary the first part of the decree seems to sustain it. "*Sub conditione* (*cum de intentione aliisque in poenitentia ad valorem requisitis dubitari debeat*) *affirmative*" makes no distinction between formal and material schismatics. The clause introduced by "*presertim*" merely indicates that if the condition therein expressed is verified, conditional absolution and extreme unction may the more readily be administered.

A fortiori, an unconscious material heretic or schismatic could be given conditional absolution.[12] Of course, whenever possible, the absolution or extreme unction, should this latter also be administered, ought to be imparted secretly, but if this cannot be done, every precaution must be taken to avoid scandal. Vermeersch advocates the administration of conditional extreme unction to an unconscious heretic or schismatic because this sacrament does not require

---

10 See Pruemmer, Manuale Mor. Theol. N. 326 who cites Linzer, Theol. Quartalschr. 1916, 693 sq.

11 Capello, De Sacramentis, Vol. 1 N. 73; Ferreres, Compendium Theol. Moral, Vol. 2, N. 608, 7.

12 Capello, l. c. N. 73.

from the subject certain acts as quasi-matter, and hence the heretic or schismatic is more apt to benefit from it than from the sacrament of penance.[13]

In the above case there is question of heretics or schismatics who are deprived of their senses. But what must be said in regard to a material heretic or schismatic who is in danger of death, but still in possession of his senses. Even in this case, according to some authors, conditional absolution may be given provided such heretics or schismatics elicit an act of contrition for their sins and are prepared to do everything ordained by God to attain eternal life.[14] Capello advances a rather ingenious explanation in support of this view. To quote his own words:

"Invaliditas et illiceitas hujusmodi absolutionis nec ex defectu intentionis nec ex carentia actuum poenitentis neque ex defectu fidei catholicae repeti potest. Non ex defectu intentionis, quia etiam in Poenitentia, sicuti in Baptismo, sufficit intentio implicita, quae profecto habetur in sincera et explicita voluntate admittendi et adhibendi omnia media a Deo ordinata ad salutem necessaria. Non ex carentia actuum poenitentis, quia, cum sufficiat ad validitatem absolutionis confessio tantum in genere facta, haec insinuari potest haeretico vel schismatico moribundo, ita ut rite confiteatur se peccatorem vel peccasse, et dein petat a Deo veniam suorum peccatorum cum spe veniae; tunc adest sive confessio sive contritio necessaria ad validitatem absolutionis. Non ex defectu fidei catholicae, quia haereticus vel schismaticus materialis bene habere potest fidem supernaturalem, ad justificationem necessariam."[15]

This opinion would appear to be confirmed by a response of the Holy Office. To the question, "An aliquando absolvi possint schmismatici materiales qui

---

13 Vermeersch, Epitome Juris Canonici T. 2, N. 16.

14 Capello, l. c. N. 73; Noldin, De Sacramentis, Vol. 3, N. 295; Ferreris, l. c. N. 608, 8; Genicot, Institutiones Theol. Moral. T. 2, N. 298.

15 Capello, l. c. N. 73.

in bona fide versantur?", it was answered, "Cum scandalum nequeat vitari, Negative, praeter mortis articulum; et tunc efficaciter remoto scandalo."[16]

This response does not distinguish between dying schismatics who are unconscious and those who, though *in articulo mortis,* still retain possession of their senses. Accordingly, it would seem that conditional absolution could be given to either of these two classes of dying schismatics.

Inasmuch as the opinions above cited are at least probable, and since in each case only *conditional* absolution or extreme unction is to be imparted, which is not prohibited by canon 731, a priest could safely follow them without exposing himself to the danger of becoming subject to the penalties of canon 2364.

Readministration of Certain Sacraments

(4) The sacraments of baptism, confirmation and holy orders, which imprint a character, cannot be repeated. If, however, a prudent doubt exists as to whether or not these sacraments have been validly administered, they should be given again *sub conditione.*[17]

Hence, indiscriminate conditional readministration of these sacraments is expressly prohibited. Each case must be considered carefully in order to determine if a prudent or reasonable doubt exists. By *prudent* here is meant any doubt whatsoever, no matter how slender, provided it is not entirely groundless, and so deserving of no consideration from an ordinarily prudent person.

Readministration of one of these sacraments without a reasonable doubt, however, would not necessarily subject the administrator to the penalties of canon 2364. For scrupulousness, or anxiety of

16 July 20, 1898.
17 Canon 732.

mind, or other mental trouble, might render the action either only lightly sinful, or perhaps not sinful at all.[18]

Baptism

(5) No infant enclosed in the maternal womb should be given baptism as long as there is a probable hope that it can be brought forth and baptized.

If the infant puts forth its head, and danger of death threatens, it should be baptized on the head, nor afterwards, if it survives, is baptism to be repeated conditionally.

But if another member appears and danger of death threatens, it is to be baptized conditionally on that member, and later, if it lives, should be given baptism again conditionally.[19]

This canon would appear to prohibit uterine baptism if a physician pronounced the delivery as probable, yet had a reasonable doubt of its fulfillment. However, according to Vermeersch, the supreme necessity of the sacrament of baptism would permit the words *probable hope* to be understood as the equivalent of moral certainty. Wherefore, if danger of death before birth is probable, an attempt could be made to baptize in the womb. This seems a rather forced interpretation of words plain in themselves. Nevertheless, the extrinsic authority of the advocate of this opinion would justify one in following it in practice.[20]

(6) Excepting the case of danger of death, it is not permitted to baptize an infant of infidels unless provision has been made for its Catholic education, and the parents or guardians, or at least one of them, give consent, or unless the child should lack parents, i. e., father, mother, grandfather, grandmother, or

---

18 Capello, l. c. N. 27.
19 Canon 746.
20 Vermeersch, l. c. N. 30.

these have forfeited their right over the child, or are not able in any way to exercise it.[21]

The rules just given for the baptism of an infidel child generally apply also to the baptism of the children of two heretics or schismatics, or of two Catholics who have fallen into apostasy or heresy or schism.[22]

In order that one may lawfully baptize an infant in danger of death it is not required that the danger be immediate. Canon 750 declares the baptism licit provided the infant is in such a condition that its death is prudently foreseen before it attains the use of reason. Accordingly, in regions rarely visited by missionaries, a priest could licitly baptize an infant despite the unwillingness of its parents if, in his prudent judgment, the child's weakened state and the unfavorableness of the climate furnished probable indications of death before the use of reason, and no better occasion for the baptism would occur in the future. But it is necessary that the danger be personal to the child. A disease ravaging the territory would not suffice to warrant an indiscriminate baptizing of all infidel infants.[23]

(7) No adult should be baptized unless, having been properly instructed, he knowingly and willingly desires baptism. Furthermore he is to be admonished to arouse a due sorrow for his sins.[24]

In danger of death, however, if he cannot receive full instruction in the principal mysteries of faith, it is sufficient for conferring baptism that in some manner he exhibit his consent to these truths and seriously promise to observe the mandates of the Christian religion.

---

21 Canon 750.

22 Canon 751.

23 Vermeersch, l. c. N. 33.

24 When there is question of baptism, those are considered adults who enjoy the use of reason, and this qualification is sufficient to enable them to ask for baptism of their own accord and to be admitted to it. Canon 745, par. 2, N. 2.

If he cannot even ask for baptism, but either previously or in his present state has manifested in some probable way an intention to receive baptism, he should be baptized conditionally; then, if he recovers, and a doubt remains concerning the validity of his baptism, baptism should be repeated conditionally.[25]

Hence, before baptizing an adult infidel who is not unconscious, the minister must ascertain whether such an infidel expressly wills to embrace the Christian religion, or to receive baptism; he must also see that he has a proper knowledge of the truths of faith; finally, he must instruct him to conceive a due sorrow for his sins.

In danger of death, moral certainty of the existence of the requisite dispositions in the infidel is not required of the minister. Even a slight probability will suffice.[26] But the priest or other minister must make some effort to instruct the dying infidel, if he still retains possession of his senses. The two following responses of the Holy Office will help to show the mind of the Church in this matter:

To the question "Utrum missionarius conferre potest baptismum in articulo mortis mahumedano adulto qui in suis erroribus supponitur in bona fide: 1. Si habeat adhuc plenam advertentiam, tantum illum adhortando ad dolorem et ad confidentiam, minime loquendo de nostris mysteriis; 2. Quamcumque habeat advertentiam, nihil ei dicendo, cum ex una parte supponitur illi non deesse contritionem, ex alia vero prudens non esse loqui cum eo de nostris mysteriis?" The Holy Office replied, ad primum et secundum, negative.[27]

To the question, "Quaeritur utrum antequam adulto conferatur baptisma minister teneatur ei explicare omnia fidei nostrae mysteria, presertim si est moribundus, quia hoc perturbaret mentem illius. An non

25 Canon 752.
26 Noldin, l. c. N. 73, 2.
27 S. C. S. O. March 30, 1898.

sufficeret si moribundus promitteret fore ut, ubi e morbo convalescat, instruendum se curet, ut in praxim redigat quod ei praescriptum fuerit?" The Holy Office answered, Ad secundum, non sufficere promissionem, sed missionarium teneri adulto etiam moribundo, qui incapax omnino non sit, explicare mysteria fidei quae sunt necessaria necessitate medii, ut sunt praecipue mysteria Trinitatis et Incarnationis.[28]

Some theologians hold that in danger of death, if an infidel has in no manner expressed or manifested his intention to receive baptism, he should not be baptized.[29] This, of course, has reference to unconscious infidels. It would seem, however, that a milder interpretation should be taken of canon 752. Genicot would not censure one who in the case of such an infidel should baptize conditionally *"fretus universali voluntate Dei salvifica, quae ad spem concipiendam de necessariis dispositionibus internis invitare videatur, dum ad moribundum ducat eum a quo externum ritum sacramentalem percipere valet."*[30] The more liberal view seems probable also to Capello who interprets canon 752 as not conclusively reprobating this practice, but merely commending a safer norm to follow. But, he adds, baptism is not to be given to such dying infidels if it entails danger of contempt of the Catholic faith to other infidels.[31] Vermeersch, too, favors this opinion. He points out that canon 752 fails to make any mention of those infidels who have given no sign of their intention. It only tells what should be done in case they have expressed some indication of a desire for baptism. Hence, since the Code is silent on this point, and does not expressly prohibit the administering of conditional baptism, one is free to baptize conditionally an infidel who has in no way manifested a wish or an intention to receive baptism.[32] Further-

28 S. C. S. O. January 25, 1703.
29 Noldin, l. c. N. 73, 2.
30 Genicot, l. c. 150.
31 Capello, l. c. N. 159.
32 Vermeersch, Summa Novi Juris Canonici, N. 288.

more, since in large cities so many have not been baptized, even though born of baptized parents, that it is difficult to determine whether or not a certain individual has received baptism, it will be expedient before imparting absolution to confer conditional baptism upon any unknown dying person who is destitute of his senses.[33]

(8) Insane persons and maniacs should not be baptized unless they have been so afflicted from birth, or before they came to the use of reason. If either of these conditions is verified, they are to be baptized as infants.

If they have lucid intervals, they are to be baptized during one of these intervals, if they so desire.

They should be baptized also in imminent danger of death, if before becoming insane they expressed a desire to receive baptism.

Those suffering from lethargy (*lethargia*) and phrenitis (*phrenesis*) are only to be baptized when they are awake and desire to receive baptism; but if danger of death threatens, they should be baptized even when not awake, provided they had manifested a desire for baptism before the attack.[34]

Even though such persons had failed at any time before their condition became dangerous to exhibit or express a wish to receive baptism, nevertheless, since conditional baptism is not expressly prohibited in such a case, its administration would not seem illicit.[35]

Confirmation

(9) A person who is not baptized cannot be validly confirmed. Besides, in order to receive confirmation licitly and fruitfully, he must be in the state

33 Vermeersch, Epitome Juris Canonici, N. 35.
34 Canon 754.
35 Vermeersch, l. c. N. 36, 4.

of grace, and if he has attained the use of reason, should also be sufficiently instructed.[36]

The Holy Eucharist

(10) The Eucharist should not be administered to children (*pueris*) who, on account of the weakness of their age, have no knowledge of or desire for this sacrament.

In danger of death Holy Communion may and should be administered to children if they are able to distinguish the Body of Christ from ordinary food, and reverently adore It.

Apart from the danger of death, a fuller knowledge of Christian Doctrine, and a more careful preparation is rightly required. The children should at least know the mysteries of faith that are necessary *necessitate medii ad salutem,* and be prepared to approach the Eucharist devoutly according to the capacity of their age.[37]

Not so many years ago an excessive rigor kept children from receiving Holy Communion until a more advanced age and rather complete instruction provided, as was thought, a suitable preparation for this august sacrament. To combat this misguided zeal the S. C. de Sacramentis on Aug. 8, 1910, declared: "Cognitio religionis quae in puero requiritur ut ipse ad Communionem convenienter se praeparet, ea est qua ipse fidei mysteria necessaria necessitate medii pro suo captu percipiat, atque Eucharisticum Panem a communi et corporali distinguat, ut ea devotione quam ipsius fert aetas, ad Sanctissimam Eucharistiam accedat." But afterwards, the pendulum swung to the opposite extreme. Hence the Code now legislates against the danger of admitting children to the Eucharist before they have acquired sufficient knowl-

---

36 Canon 786.

37 Canon 854.

edge of their religion. Canon 854 stipulates certain conditions to be observed in the matter of instruction for first Holy Communion. But who is to judge of the fitness of the child? The Code seems to divide authority between the parents, the confessor, and the pastor without, however, assigning to any one of these three the final decision. Canon 854, par. 4, states that judgment concerning the fitness of a child to receive First Communion pertains to the confessor and the parents, or those who are in the place of the parents. But par. 5 of the same canon gives to the pastor the office of watching over the aspirants to Holy Communion. Moreover, he is empowered to subject them to an examination, if he prudently deems this expedient, to determine whether they have reached the use of reason, or have the required dispositions. What, then, could, or should be done in the event of a conflict of opinion between the pastor and the confessor or parents? Would the priest of another parish be justified in giving First Holy Communion to a child whose pastor declared him unfit, but whose parents and confessor pronounced as worthy to receive the Sacrament? Vermeersch thinks that the pastor should have authority over the parents, but that there is no obligation imposed by law upon the parents to obey him in this respect.[38] It would seem that in his own parish a pastor could refuse Communion to one who, in his judgment, lacked the necessary qualities, even though the confessor and parents had passed a favorable judgment. But he could not prevent the child from approaching the Sacred Table in another parish.[39]

Another difficulty may arise in the application of this canon from the fact that those who habitually lack the use of reason are regarded as infants.[40] Accordingly, it would appear that even to those

---

38 Vermeersch, l. c. N. 118.
39 Capello, l. c. N. 530.
40 Canon 88, par. 3.

persons who became insane after once attaining the use of discretion the Eucharist should be denied as long as they remain in their unnatural state, or have no lucid intervals. This deduction seems to derive confirmation from the instructions on this point of the Roman Ritual:

"Amentibus praeterea et phreneticis communicare non licet; licebit, tamen, si quando habeant lucida intervalla et devotionem ostendunt, dum in eo statu manent, si nullum indignitatis periculum adsit."[41]

These words appear to exclude the Eucharist to such insane persons even *in articulo mortis.* While some authors hold this view, nevertheless theologians commonly interpret the Ritual as prohibiting ordinary Communion and not Viaticum. Wherefore, if it can reasonably be presumed that these *amentes* had at one time at least an implicit intention of receiving the Eucharist, and that they are in the state of grace, and provided proper precautions are taken against the danger of irreverence, it is licit to give them Viaticum, even should their derangement persist *in articulo mortis.*[42]

Other questions bearing on the insane and others similarly afflicted are discussed in the various manuals of Moral Theology.

(11) The Eucharist must be refused to the publicly unworthy, such as excommunicates, interdicted persons, and those manifestly *infames,* unless there is evidence of their penitence and amendment, and they have made due reparation for the public scandal.

If occult sinners privately ask for Holy Communion and the minister knows their impenitence, they should be refused; but if they request It publicly, and scandal would result from a refusal, It must be given them.[43]

---

41 Roman Ritual, Title 4, chapter 1, N. 10.

42 Noldin, l. c. N. 135 e; Capello, l. c. N. 463; Ferreres, l. c. N. 425; Genicot, l. c. N. 190.

43 Canon 855.

The enumeration of the publicly unworthy in this canon is made only *demonstrative,* and not *taxative,* that is, the Code merely wishes to furnish some examples of unworthiness, and not to limit the publicly unfit to those expressly mentioned. Hence, *meretrices, concubinarii, exercentes professionem notorie illicitam, munus publico decreto prohibitum,* even though not technically declared *infames,* must be considered as *publici indigni.*

If the crime is public elsewhere, but not in the place where Communion is requested, on account of the danger of scandal of the faithful the Sacrament should probably not be withheld, unless it were foreseen that future divulgation of the sin would cause greater offence to the people.[44]

Those persons also should be repelled who are immodestly dressed when they approach the altar rail, especially if previously a general warning had been issued. They, however, are not refused on the score of public unworthiness, but rather as *importuni et inurbani petitores.*[45]

It should also be noted that repentance alone does not suffice to gain readmittance to the Eucharistic Table. The Code requires also reparation of the public scandal. In some cases, public approach to the tribunal of penance will be sufficient. In other more flagrant ones, it might be necessary either to retract impious doctrine, or to give up the occasion of sin.[46]

If a person were publicly branded *infamis,* to effect which there is need of a declaration from the Ordinary,[47] his repentance and satisfaction alone will not warrant a priest in readmitting him to the Eucharist. For judgment in this case is reserved to the Ordinary.[48]

---

44 Vermeersch, l. c. N. 117.
45 Vermeersch, l. c. N. 117.
46 Noldin, l. c. N. 37.
47 Canon 2293.
48 Canon 2295.

(12) One who has received the Eucharist on a certain day may not receive It again on that day unless there is urgent danger of death, or need of preventing irreverence towards the Blessed Sacrament.[49]

(13) A person who has not fasted from midnight must not be given Communion, unless there is pressing danger of death, or necessity of safeguarding the Holy Eucharist from indignity.

Sick people, however, who have been confined (*decumbentes*) for a month without certain hope of a speedy recovery, with the prudent counsel of their confessor, may receive the Eucharist once or twice a week, although they have taken previously some medicine, or something *per modum potus*.[50]

The New Law introduces a change in respect to sick persons who may receive Holy Communion without fasting. By a decree of Pius X through the Sacred Congregation of the Council sick people who had taken something *per modum potus* could be given the Eucharist twice a month.[51] The decree made no mention of medicine, which is now allowed by the Code. Only in the event of their residing in a house in which the Blessed Sacrament was reserved, or Mass could be celebrated, were they permitted to receive twice a week. Now the new legislation grants the privilege of communicating twice a week to all sick persons without distinction, provided the requisite conditions are fulfilled.

Since par. 2 of this canon posits an exception to the general law contained in par. 1, it ought to bear a strict interpretation. Accordingly, *decumbunt* should be understood literally. Canonists, however, generally take it in a broad sense. This, perhaps, is due to their considering par. 2 not an exception, but part of the general law. Their attitude is supported by a dec-

---

49 Canon 857.
50 Canon 858.
51 Dec. 7, 1906.

laration of the Sacred Congregation of the Council, according to which *decumbentes* would include those who were not able to lie in bed, or could arise from it several hours during the day.[52] Some hold that a continuous confinement in the bedroom or house suffices. Genicot claims that practically such a confinement will not exist unless it is necessary to administer the Eucharist in the bedroom.[53] Vermeersch and Capello require even less. They would give Communion to a sick person not fasting, if the stipulated conditions were fulfilled, even though he should be able to visit a church to receive.[54] Noldin opposes this view on the score of its tendency to relax the strictness of the Eucharistic fast.[55] Capello, on the contrary, thinks (*indubitanter putamus*) that provided the conditions laid down by the Lawgiver are carefully observed, danger of relaxation of the law of fasting is obviated. There seems no conclusive reason to reject this opinion. At least, it is not in clear contradiction to the decree above cited. Rather, as Capello remarks, it is more in conformity with the mind of the Lawgiver who desires in every way possible to refresh the sick with the food of life.

The following are the conditions to which the concession of this canon is subject:

(A) That the person be truly sick. Sickness could be due to old age, disease, debility, or any other real infirmity. A serious or dangerous disease is not required.

(B) The sickness must have already lasted a month. Capello interprets this broadly. He holds it as certain that 26 or 27 days would be sufficient time. It should be noted that the faculty is not extended to those whose infirmity is just beginning, even though

---

52 March 6, 1907.
53 Genicot, l. c. 202.
54 Vermeersch, l. c. 124; Capello, l. c. N. 506.
55 Noldin, l. c. N. 157 b.

it is of such a character that it will certainly continue for a month.

(C) That there be no certain hope of a quick recovery. The words "certain hope" manifestly imply more than a mere conjecture or probability. There ought to be a moral certainty. "*Cito*" signifies about three or four days.

(D) The sick person must receive permission from his confessor.

(E) The confessor may grant the privilege for only twice in a week. Capello asserts it would be a grave offence to communicate three or four times a week. However, there is no reason why the sick person could not receive on other days, if he observed the fast, especially if this entailed some personal inconvenience. In order to use the privilege inability to fast is not required. But if the *infirmus* can fast without any inconvenience he should be exhorted to receive the Sacrament fasting. Vermeersch observes that a prudent confessor will not give his consent to one who is easily able to keep the fast.

(F) Medicine, or something *per modum potus,* is allowed. The medicine may be solid. But it must be taken primarily to counteract or destroy some disease, and not merely for the purpose of strengthening the bodily powers. What is meant *per modum potus?* This question was answered by a declaration of the Holy Office:[56]

"Mens est, ut liceat sumere jusculum, caffaeum, lac, aut alium cibum liquidum, etsi ei sit permixta substantia aliqua, ex. gratia, leves pastilli farinae (semolino), panis radula tritus (pangrattato), ovum dilutum, etc.: dummodo mixtio non amittat naturam cibi liquidi."

It is commonly admitted that a cooked egg is food. As to an uncooked egg, or one in its natural state, some moralists consider it as food.[57] Yet it would

56 Sept. 7, 1897.

57 Gennari, Quistioni Teologico Morali, N. 195.

seem to be consumed *per modum potus.* Capello and Vermeersch embrace this opinion. Capello draws a distinction. If the egg is sucked slowly (*guttatim*), *undoubtedly* it is to be held as *potus.* If taken otherwise, provided it is not at all cooked, *probably* it is a liquid.

Extreme Unction

(14) Only those of the faithful who have come to the use of reason and are in danger of death from sickness or old age should be given extreme unction.

This sacrament cannot be repeated in the same illness, unless the sick person after being anointed should recover and his condition again become dangerous.[58]

(15) Extreme unction is not to be administered to those who impenitently, stubbornly and manifestly continue in mortal sin; but if a doubt exists, it should be given conditionally.[59]

Noldin claims that by virtue of this canon those persons should not be anointed when unconscious who, while in possession of their senses, stubbornly rejected the sacraments of the Church. His reason is that they do not furnish even a probable hope of an intention to receive this sacrament.[60] Genicot, on the other hand, holds that probably extreme unction could be given conditionally to them. For, he says, they can be presumed with some likelihood of truth to have elicited an internal act of contrition. But he qualifies this opinion with the caution that often it will be necessary to refrain from anointing such persons until they have shown some sign of repentance, especially if many would see or learn of the

---

58 Canon 940.
59 Canon 942.
60 Noldin, l. c. 444 c.

action, in order to avoid bringing contempt upon the sacraments.[61]

Genicot's opinion seems more probable. For, as Vermeersch notes, we cannot be sure of contumaciousness in the case of one deprived of his senses.[62] Even though, to all outward appearances, a person be incapable of a rational act, yet it is not absolutely certain that the mind is not active, and that he does not desire the sacraments.

Holy Orders

(16) Only a baptized male can validly receive ordination; one cannot licitly receive orders unless, in the judgment of his Ordinary, he possesses the requisite qualities in accordance with the canons of the Code, and be not bound by any irregularity or other impediment.[63] The qualities which the aspirant to orders should have are set forth in canons 969, 973, 974, 975, 976, 979. The irregularities which render an ordination illicit, unless a dispensation is secured, are contained in canons 984 and 985. Canon 987 declares the simple impediments to ordination.[64]

The sacrament of matrimony of course does not fall under the provisions of canon 2364. For in matrimony the contracting parties are the ministers of the sacrament.

PENALTY: The determinate penalty specified for a violation of canon 2364 is suspension from administering the sacraments for a time to be prudently determined by the Ordinary. This penalty is a vindictive one and not a censure. For it does not terminate with the cessation of contumacy, but is to last for a period prudently fixed by the Ordinary.

---

61 Genicot, l. c. N. 423.

62 Vermeersch, l. c. N. 226.

63 Canon 968.

64 See Hickey "Irregularities and Simple Impediments in the New Code."

It is also stated that other punishments should be inflicted in addition to the suspension, if the gravity of the fault requires severer treatment. For instance, a case of relapse would warrant the Ordinary in taking extra measures against an offender. Or if the offence were particularly flagrant it might merit sterner punishment. No limit is placed on the penal power of the Ordinary in this regard, except that the penalties should correspond to the seriousness of the delinquency.

Other punishments imposed by law against crimes of this kind retain their force. Canon 2364 is a general one and not intended to exclude other particular sanctions. An example of one of these special penalties is canon 2373, which relates to ordinations.

The penalty is ferendae sententiae. Moreover, the words *ausus fuerit* indicate that there should be full knowledge and complete deliberation on the part of the culprit.

CHAPTER II

CONFIRMATION

The Church at different times has decreed severe punishments against those of her priests who presumed to perform a function reserved to bishops. In 494 Gelasius 1 declared that priests who exercised a power especially pertaining to the episcopal ministry should suffer an immediate deprivation of the dignity of the priesthood and of sacred communion.[1] This was only a repetition of similar legislation by the Council of Sardica in 343.[2] The Second Council of Braga also in 563 prohibited to priests under pain of deposition of office what the former canons forbade in this matter.[3]

When the need arose simple priests have received a special faculty to confirm. But generally within certain limits. Greek priests as a rule give confirmation without a special delegation, and their ministration is accepted by the Western Church as valid. But they, too, may not use this power indiscriminately. On Oct. 6, 1863, the S. C. Prop. de Fide issued a decree in which the practice of certain Rutheno-Catholic priests of confirming children of the Latin rite immediately after giving them baptism in cases of necessity or inconvenience was condemned and forbidden under penalty of an *ipso facto* suspension *a divinis*.[4]

In the New Law canon 2365 states that a priest who, without the requisite power obtained either *a jure* or by a special concession of the Roman Pontiff, would presume to administer the sacrament of con-

---

1 Gelasius 1, Ep. ad Ep. Lucan. cap. 6 (Thiel Ep. R. P., p. 365 sq.).
2 Hefele, History of the Councils, T. 1, p. 601.
3 Hefele, l. c. T. 2, p. 80.
4 Collectanea S. Cong. de Prop. Fide, N. 1243 C.

firmation should be suspended. If he had received the faculty, but dared to go beyond its limits, he would *ipso facto* lose the power granted him.

These penalties are based on canon 782. Par. 1 of this canon declares that the ordinary minister of confirmation is the bishop only;

Par. 2, that the extraordinary minister is a priest to whom by common law or special indult of the Apostolic See this faculty has been granted;

Par. 4, that a priest of the Latin rite, to whom by virtue of an indult this power belongs, validly confirms only the faithful of his own rite, unless the indult expressly decrees otherwise;

Par. 5, that it is unlawful, or is forbidden (*nefas est*) to priests of the Oriental rite who have the faculty or privilege of conferring confirmation upon infants of their own rite immediately after baptism to confirm infants of the Latin rite.

A priest who did not at all possess the faculty of confirming and yet attempted to confirm, should suffer a general suspension, that is, should be suspended both from office and benefice.[5] The penalty is *ferendae sententiae,* and calls for full knowledge and deliberation on the part of the delinquent (*ausus fuerit*). Moreover, it is not a vindictive punishment, but a censure.[6] It is not reserved.

The second part of canon 2365 provides the penalty for a violation of the implicit prohibition of canon 782, par. 4 noted above. A priest guilty of this fault, or of going beyond the limits of his special faculties in any other way, would lose *ipso facto* the power granted him. The deprivation is *latae sententiae,* and inasmuch as presumption is required (*praesumpserit*), any diminution of imputability whatsoever, whether on the part of the intellect or the will, would excuse one from incurring it.[7]

---

5 Canon 2278.
6 Canon 2255.
7 Canon 2229.

Greek priests, however, who act against the provisions of par. 5 of canon 782 by confirming infants of the Latin rite immediately after baptizing them do not suffer this punishment. For the Code legislates only for the Latin Church, unless the nature of the case would demand inclusion of the Orientals. Hence, we must look elsewhere for the sanction of this prohibition. It is found in the decree of the S. C. Prop. Fide of Oct. 6, 1863, cited above, which orders an *ipso facto* suspension *a divinis* for such an offence.

CHAPTER III

HEARING CONFESSIONS WITHOUT JURISDICTION

Jurisdiction *in foro sacramentali* is the power by which a priest can pronounce sentence on those subject to him by remitting or retaining sins. It is necessary for the validity of sacramental absolution. Formerly, approbation, or the declaration by the bishop of the fitness of a priest to hear confessions, was also a requisite for validity. Now, however, the Code requires only the power of orders and jurisdiction. This change is reflected in canon 2366 which declares a penalty for hearing confessions without jurisdiction, and makes no mention of approbation. Approbation finds expression in canon 877, which states that local Ordinaries shall not grant jurisdiction, nor the religious superior jurisdiction or license to hear confessions, except to such as have been found fit upon examination, unless there should be question of a priest of whose theological knowledge they have evidence from other sources.

Two new censures are introduced in canon 2366. The first is suspension *a divinis* incurred *ipso facto* by a priest who presumes to hear sacramental confessions without the necessary jurisdiction. In order to incur this penalty it is not necessary that absolution be imparted. Sacramental confession on the part of the penitent suffices, that is, that the penitent should tell his sins to the priest lacking jurisdiction with the hope or expectation of obtaining absolution. It might happen that due to a common error on the part of the faithful the Church would supply jurisdiction and the absolution be valid. Nevertheless, the priest would incur the suspension if he acted with full knowledge and deliberation, because the Church supplies jurisdiction in this case for the good of the faithful, and not to aid a delinquent priest to escape the penalties due to his malice.[1] Hence, according to Farrugia, if a priest while hearing confessions should recall with moral certainty that the time of his jurisdiction had expired, he would be obliged to discontinue hearing until he had obtained express jurisdiction. If he should continue hearing the confessions without first having secured the necessary jurisdiction, he would incur the censure.[2] (Of course, presumption is required.) Chelodi implies the same.[3] Noldin, however, would permit the confessor to remain in the confessional. To quote his own words:

"Sacerdos, qui confessiones audit et absolvit postquam tempus jurisdictionis jam expiravit; . . . . fruuntur errore communi. Quare, is qui confessiones audiens recordaretur tempus jurisdictionis jam elapsum esse, vel de hac re dubitaret, ab excipiendis confessionibus cessare non deberet."[4]

He makes the fact that jurisdiction is supplied on account of common error the reason why a confessor should continue hearing confessions even after he recalls that the time of his jurisdiction has elapsed. But this, at least in ordinary cases, i. e., in which no danger of scandal threatens from the departure of the confessor, does not seem to be the intention of the law. Rather, as Chelodi states, "The Church supplies jurisdiction for the sake of the faithful, and does not grant it in favor of the priest."

This censure affects priests only, religious or secular, and not deacons, other clerics, or laymen who might fraudulently hear confessions. Nor do bishops fall under its scope. For they are not subject to penalties *latae sententiae* of suspension or interdict unless they are expressly mentioned.[5]

---

1 Chelodi, Jus Poenale, N. 89.
2 Farrugia, Commentarium in Censuras Latae Sententiae, N. 291.
3 Chelodi, l. c. N. 89.
4 Noldin, l. c. N. 346.
5 Canon 2227.

The penalty incurred is *suspensio a divinis.* This suspension forbids any act of the power of orders which one has received either by ordination or by special privilege. An example of the latter would be the power granted to a priest to administer confirmation.

The suspension is not reserved. To contract it presumption is required. Hence, the priest must know that he lacks jurisdiction, and also that he is forbidden to hear the confession under pain of suspension. Crass, but not affected ignorance, would excuse from the penalty.

Jurisdiction for Confessions of Female Religious

Practically speaking, the laws governing the acquisition and possession of sacramental jurisdiction will cause little or no difficulty. As a rule, the priest will know when he possesses jurisdiction. A doubt, however, may arise in respect to the confessions of female religious. For in this connection the New Law has introduced a change that is apt to beget some confusion.

Before the New Code a female religious for the peace of her conscience could make a valid and licit confession in a church, public, or semi-public oratory *extra propriam domum* to any confessor approved by the local Ordinary for hearing the confessions of women.[6] Canon 522 reproduces this legislation with one exception. The words "*extra propriam domum*" have been omitted. Wherefore, if follows that if there is a church, public, or semi-public oratory *intra propriam domum,* a religious could for the peace of her conscience make use of canon 522 there also.

Some authors have given this canon a rather strict interpretation. Fanfani, for instance, states:

6 Decree of S. Cong. de Religiosis, Feb. 3, 1913.

"Verba canonis 'in qualibet ecclesia vel oratorio etiam semi-publico' intelligenda esse, ut nobis videtur, etiam de ecclesia et oratorio propriis; dummodo id fiat ad modum saecularium mulierum, in confessionali publico seu communi, et tempore quo ipsae saeculares mulieres possent, si velint, ad talem confessarium accedere. Ubi enim lex non distinguit, nec nos distinguere debemus. Nihilominus quod supradictae conditiones verificentur necessarium omnino videtur: secus, si cuilibet religiosae, semper ac habet possibilitatem, liceret quemcumque confessarium pro mulieribus approbatum, in propria ecclesia seu oratorio etiam semi-publico, quocumque tempore et in ipso confessionali pro sororibus deputato adire, actum esset de confessariis ordinariis et extraordinariis pro ipsis."[7]

This interpretation, however, appears too severe when considered in the light of a response to a doubt proposed to the Pontifical Commission for the authentic interpretation of the canons of the Code. The doubt submitted was, "Utrum verba canonis 522: confessio in qualibet ecclesia vel oratorio etiam semi-publico peracta valida et licita est: ita intelligenda sint, ut confessio extra ea loca peracta non tantum illicita, sed etiam invalida sit."

The Commission answered as follows: "Canon 522 ita est intelligendus, ut confessiones, quas ad suae conscientiae tranquillitatem religiosae peragunt apud confessarium ab Ordinario loci approbatum, licitae et validae sint, dummodo fiant in ecclesia vel oratorio etiam semi-publico, aut in loco ad audiendas confessiones mulierum legitime destinato."[8]

The words of the above response "*aut in loco ad audiendas confessiones mulierum legitime destinato*" indicate that the Lawgiver intended a liberal interpretation of canon 522. Not only is it not necessary that the confessions be heard at a time when opportunity is offered to lay persons also to make their

---

7 Fanfani, De Jure Religiosorum, N. 110.
8 November 24, 1920.

confessions, but it is not even required that the sacrament always be administered in the place in which confessionals have been erected. To understand clearly the significance of the phrase "*in loco ad audiendas confessiones legitime destinato*," we must consult canons 909 and 910. According to canon 909, "Sedes confessionalis ad audiendas mulierum confessiones semper collocetur in loco patenti et conspicuo, et generatim in ecclesia vel oratorio publico aut semipublico mulieribus destinato. Sedes confessionalis crate fixa ac tenuiter perforata inter poenitentem et confessarium sit instructa."

Hence, ordinarily, the confession should be made in the confessional where the sisters regularly approach the Sacred Tribunal.

But according to canon 910, "Feminarum confessiones extra sedem confessionalem ne audiantur, nisi ex causa infirmitatis aliave verae necessitatis et adhibitis cautelis quas Ordinarius loci opportunas judicaverit."

Accordingly, if a case of necessity should arise, if, for example, a nun or sister desired to confess "*ad tranquillitatem conscientiae*" to a visiting priest, and at that very time workmen were engaged in making repairs to the chapel, or for some other good reason it was inexpedient to resort to the chapel, the priest could licitly hear the confession in the parlor.

It is disputed whether the phrase "*ad tranquillitatem conscientiae*" demands the presence of some special trouble of conscience for the validity of the confession. Until an authentic decision solves this doubt, it is safe to follow the opinion of those who maintain that the words are not *ad validitatem*.[9]

---

9 Motry, Diocesan Faculties According to the Code, p. 95.

CHAPTER IV

ABSOLVING FROM RESERVED SINS WITHOUT JURISDICTION

The second new censure decreed by canon 2366 is suspension from hearing confessions incurred *ipso facto* by a priest who presumes to absolve from reserved sins without the necessary jurisdiction.

Note that there is question here not of reserved censures, but of reserved sins. Other penalties are provided for absolution from reserved censures by one lacking the requisite faculties.

To reserve a sin signifies the restriction of a confessor's power to absolve from that sin by his superior who, as it were, calls the sin to his own judgment.

Some changes have been made by the New Law in respect to those affected by reservations of sins.

Before the promulgation of the Code it was disputed whether a *peregrinus* was bound by the reservations of the place in which he confessed. The generally received view was that a confessor could absolve a *peregrinus* from sins reserved in the diocese of the confessor unless the sin was also reserved in the diocese of the penitent. But after the Code appeared many theologians held that a *peregrinus* could not be absolved in a strange diocese, no matter whether the sin was reserved in his own diocese or not.[1] Still the matter remained uncertain, but a reply to a query on this point made by Cardinal Logue to the Pontifical Commission for interpreting the Code of Canon Law conclusively settled all doubts. The question was, "Whether a peregrinus is bound by the

---

1 Noldin, l. c. N. 364 e; Ferreres, l. c. N. 674; Genicot, l. c. N. 349.

reservations of the place in which he is located?" On August 17, 1919, the Commission replied "*Affirmative.*"[2]

Canon 900 treats of cessation of reservations of sins.[3] It decrees that all reservations cease.

(1) When those who confess are sick people who are not able to leave the house, or "*sponsi*" about to be married.

(2) As often as the lawful superior refuses the faculty asked for in a particular case, or when, according to the prudent judgment of the confessor, the faculty cannot be asked of the lawful superior without great inconvenience to the penitent, or without danger of violating the sacramental seal.

(3) Outside the territory of the one who has reserved the case, even though the penitent has repaired thither solely for the purpose of obtaining absolution.

In the Old Law it was held that a stranger who left his diocese in order to obtain absolution from a reserved sin "*in fraudem legis,*" that is, to evade the judgment of his superior, could not be absolved from that sin in the diocese to which he repaired. Now par. 3 of canon 900, quoted above, declares that such a *peregrinus* is entitled to absolution.

It was also held in the Old Law that if a superior unjustly denied a confessor's request for faculties, the confessor could not absolve his penitent from the reserved sin.[4] Now, according to par. 2 of canon 900, in the event of a refusal on the part of a superior to grant the desired faculty, the confessor is free to absolve.

---

2 Irish Eccl. Record, Vol. XIV, July to Dec. 1919.

3 Vermeersch, l. c. N. 179, observes that canon 900 pertains only to sins which are reserved without censure. The adjective "*quaevis*" indicates that it would apply also to the only sin reserved *ratione sui* to the Holy See, viz., false accusation of an innocent priest of solicitation made "*apud judices ecclesiasticos.*" Canon 894.

4 Noldin, l. c. p. 434 (1914).

Special Faculties of Pastors, Those Who are in the Place of Pastors, and Missionaries

According to canon 899, par. 3, pastors, and all those who go in law by the name of pastors, can absolve *ipso jure,* that is, without any delegation or express concession, from cases which the Ordinary has reserved in any manner to himself during the whole time assigned for fulfilling the paschal precept, whether it be the usual period of time, or an extension of it made by the Ordinary. Missionaries also enjoy the same power during the time of a mission.

Pastors are defined in canon 451, where it is also laid down that quasi-pastors, who govern quasi-parishes, and parochial vicars, if they are endowed with full parochial power, in law go by the name of pastors.

Quasi-pastors, as ascertained from canon 216, par. 3, are those set over the territorial divisions of vicariates and prefectures apostolic.

According to Blat, the following are parochial vicars possessed of full parochial power, and so included among those enumerated in canon 899, par. 3:

1. *Vicarius simpliciter dictus,* who is the vicar of a parish *pleno jure* united to a religious house, a chapter church, or another moral person, according to the provisions of canon 471.

2. *Vicarius oeconomus,* who is appointed to a vacant parish by the Ordinary, as stipulated in canons 472-473.

3. *Vicarius substitutus,* who takes the place of an absent pastor, as provided for in canon 474.

4. *Vicarius adjutor,* who assists the pastor unfit to perform his duties through old age, etc., in accordance with canon 475. Blat, however, makes a distinction in his case. He says that if the *adjutor*

takes the place of the pastor in all things, in which event all the rights and duties of a pastor belong to him except the application of the *Missa pro populo,* which obligates the pastor, as is set forth in canon 475, par. 2, then, notwithstanding the fact that he is not obliged to apply the *Missa pro populo,* he is endowed with full parochial powers, and so goes in law by the name of pastor. But this would not be the case should he only partly assist the pastor.

As to the *vicarius cooperator,* or as he is more commonly designated, *curate,* who is assigned to help a pastor when the latter is unable alone to take proper care of his parish on account of the large number of his flock, or for other reasons, Blat states that such a vicar generally is not endowed with full parochial power, and so does not go under the name of pastor in law.[5] Hence, he cannot take advantage of the provisions of canon 899, par. 3.

Two things of special significance must be noted in respect to canon 899. First, that, just as in canon 900, there is question of sins and not of censures. And second, that it does not specify all reserved sins, but only those three or four which the Ordinary may reserve by and to himself. Accordingly, it would not apply to the reservation of the sin committed by making a false charge of solicitation to the ecclesiastical judges against an innocent priest. For this reservation is made by the Code itself to the Holy See. Nor would it apply to any sins that might be reserved to the Ordinary by law. But suppose the Ordinary reserved to himself a censure of excommunication against a certain offence. According to canon 2246, reserved censures that impede reception of the sacraments, i. e., excommunication and personal interdict, include also reservation of the sin to which the censure is attached. Could pastors and missionaries by virtue of canon 899 absolve from such reserved

---

5 Blat, De Personis, p. 509 foll.

sins during the specified times? Before answering this question we must consider canon 2250, par. 2. Here it is stated that if there is question of a censure which hinders reception of the sacraments, the person under such a censure may not be absolved from his sins until he first obtains absolution from the censure. (This, though, refers only to the licitness of the absolution.)[6] Hence, in the case under discussion, pastors and missionaries could not licitly grant absolution from the sin reserved *ratione censurae* before removal of the censure. If the case were urgent and the censure involved were *latae sententiae*, of course canon 2254 could be used. In that event, together with absolution of the censure, reservation of the sin would automatically cease.[7]

PENALTY: Sole claims that to incur the penalty for absolving from reserved sins without jurisdiction there must be pronunciation of the form of absolution.[8] Ayrinhac goes further. He says that besides pronouncing the form the confessor must have the intention of absolving, because simulation of absolution is not mentioned here as in the canon following, which deals with absolution of an accomplice *in peccato turpi*.[9] This would seem to be correct, inasmuch as penal laws are subject to a strict interpretation.

Ayrinhac also holds that the law does not apply to sins reserved *ratione censurae,* but only to those reserved *ratione sui.* This is likewise the view held by the Irish Theological Quarterly.[10] Chelodi says otherwise. He asserts that the penalty is incurred by a priest who presumes to absolve from a sin reserved by reason of a censure, and also that if the censure were one reserved in a special or very special manner, the delinquent confessor would become

---

6 Capello, l. c. p. 28; Chelodi, l. c. p. 36.
7 Canon 2246.
8 Sole, De Delictis et Poenis, N. 421.
9 Ayrinhac—Penal Legislation in the New Code, p. 315.
10 Irish Theological Quarterly, January, 1918.

subject to two penalties, the one decreed by canon 2338 for undue absolution from these reserved censures, and the other enacted by canon 2366 for such absolution from reserved sins.[11]

Ayrinhac's view, however, must be taken as the true one for the reason that reservation of a sin *ratione censurae* merely prevents the licit absolution of that sin. Hence, although a confessor without the requisite faculties would illicitly absolve from such a sin, yet his absolution would be valid, and so, given with jurisdiction. Accordingly, he could not be said to have presumed to absolve from a reserved sin without jurisdiction, which is required in order to incur the penalty of canon 2365.

The suspension is not reserved. Moreover, presumption is required. Wherefore, even crass ignorance of the law or penalty would excuse a priest from incurring it.

---

11 Chelodi, l. c. N. 89.

CHAPTER V

ABSOLUTION OF AN ACCOMPLICE

It is surely not fitting that a priest absolve his accomplice in sin. This is true, indeed, of any sin at all, but in respect to a sin against the sixth commandment, it would be both heinously criminal and extremely dangerous because of the deep irreverence thereby shown to the sacrament of penance, and the incitement to future sin contained in the easy accusation of the crime. Hence, the Church forbids under the most severe penalties a confessor to absolve his accomplice *in peccato turpi.*

Until about the middle of the 18th century, theologians commonly maintained the validity of absolution imparted to an accomplice *in peccato turpi.* Many also asserted its liceity if each offender had duly repented of his crime, and there was no danger of further sin. Marchant held that it was forbidden neither by divine nor natural law, because, on the one hand, the priest could be truly contrite and confer the sacrament, and on the other, the penitent could have true contrition for his sin.[1]

But by particular statute jurisdiction at times had been taken from a priest to absolve his accomplice *contra sextum.* St. Charles Borromeo forbade his priests to absolve any accomplice at all, even if the sin of complicity were not *in materia turpi.*[2] It remained, however, for Benedict XIV to enact the first general legislation on this subject. It was contained in his constitution *"Sacramentum Poenitentiae"* of June 1, 1741. As was to be expected this first law did not cover all phases of the question. Benedict XIV himself, realizing this, supplemented it by two other

1 Hortus Pastorum, p. 485.

2 Cavigioli, De Censuris Latae Sententiae, N. 71.

constitutions, the "*Apostolici Muneris*" of Feb. 8, 1745, and the "*Inter Praeteritos,*" of Dec. 3, 1749. Pius IX embodied this legislation in his constitution, "*Apostolicae Sedis.*" Moreover, it has been officially interpreted by several decrees of Congregations and Tribunals, particularly by those of the Holy Office, May 23, 1873 and Dec. 10, 1883, and of the Sacred Penitentiary, March 1, 1878 and Feb. 19, 1896. Finally, canon 2367 of the New Law contains substantially the legislation of the two pontiffs together with some of the decisions of the Congregations and Tribunals.

In his first constitution "*Sacramentum Poenitentiae,*" Benedict XIV declared that outside a case of necessity, i. e., *in articulo mortis,* and provided no other priest were present who could fulfill the office of confessor, no priest should hear the confession of his accomplice *in peccato turpi.* Furthermore, such a priest had no jurisdiction over his accomplice for absolving from a sin of this kind. Absolution, if imparted, was declared to be invalid, and if the confessor had acted presumptuously, he *ipso facto* incurred the penalty of a greater (*majoris*) excommunication reserved to Benedict XIV and his successors only.

But this legislation was not complete. It was too general and did not provide for several contingencies that might arise. Accordingly, Benedict XIV himself in his constitution "*Apostolici Muneris*" made some additions to the previous constitution. It was stated that a priest could validly, indeed, but not licitly, absolve his accomplice at the time of death if another priest were present who could grant the absolution, "even if this second priest should not be approved for hearing confessions." But recognizing that perhaps there might be grave danger either to the delinquent priest or his accomplice in absolutely requiring the services of this other priest who should chance to be at hand or could easily be summoned, it was decreed that if this other priest could not be called without danger of infamy or scandal, then he should be regarded as if not present, and the first priest should give the absolution to his accomplice.

Canonists in interpreting the above concession commonly hold that in danger of death a priest excommunicated or suspended by a condemnatory or declaratory sentence does not have the preference over the priest accomplice. Capello rightly observes that such a priest generally cannot be summoned without some danger of scandal or infamy.[3]

Although both the Old and the New Law lay down "*in articulo mortis*" as the time when a priest under certain conditions may validly and licitly absolve his accomplice, yet the common opinion interprets this as also meaning "*periculum mortis.*"[4] This opinion is confirmed by a consideration of canon 884 of the New Code which implicitly asserts the licitness of absolution given to an accomplice in a case of necessity "*in periculo mortis.*"

What is meant by "*periculum mortis*"? According to Chelodi, it signifies when death is truly probable, whether intrinsically, as, e. g., from disease, a wound, difficult parturition, or extreme old age, or extrinsically, as, from war,[5] a dangerous voyage, etc.[6]

D'Annibale extends it even to the case in which a person is in danger of becoming perpetually insane.[7] Capello approves and embraces this opinion.[8]

It is also a very probable opinion, and one maintained by several eminent authors, that although only danger of death is mentioned for this matter, nevertheless a case of extreme necessity would also

---

3 Capello, l. c. p. 55.

4 Capello, l. c. p. 55; Chelodi, l. c. N. 90; Cavigioli, l. c. N. 76; Pennachi, Commentarium in Const. Apost. Sedis, Vol. 2, p. 334.

5 "Miles quicumque in statu bellicae convocationis, seu, ut aiunt, mobilitationis, constitutus, ipso facto aequiparari potest iis qui versantur in periculo mortis, ita ut a quovis obvio sacerdote possit absolvi." S. Penitent. March 18, 1912 and May 29, 1915.

6 Chelodi, l. c. N. 35.

7 Commentarium in Const. Apost. Sedis, p. 152.

8 Capello, p. 33, footnote 1.

suffice.[9] Pennachi advances a very cogent reason in support of this view. He says "Benedict XIV granted the faculty to a confessor to absolve his accomplice at the hour of death if otherwise infamy or scandal could not be avoided; the danger of infamy was, therefore, the chief and only reason which induced the Pope to moderate the rigor of his law. Accordingly, Benedict desired to avoid scandal of the faithful and infamy of the priest. Hence, if in some case this reason should most certainly be present, I think a priest who would absolve his accomplice would not act against the law."[10]

Pius IX in his constitution "*Apostolicae Sedis*" practically reproduced the law of Benedict XIV. He, however, omitted the words "*ausus fuerit.*" And so from this time a priest even without presumption could incur the penalty. Consequently, it was declared later that crass or supine ignorance would not suffice to excuse from the punishment.[11] For a violation of the law the penalty was decreed to be excommunication reserved in a special manner to the Roman Pontiff. This reservation, however, was really one reserved in a most special manner. This is clear from two declarations of the Holy Office.[12] For in the general and very ample concession of faculties for absolving from all cases, even those reserved in a special manner, given by these declarations, this case of absolution of an accomplice was expressly excepted.[13]

But since the "*Apostolicae Sedis*" had referred only to those who absolve (*absolventes*), commentators of this constitution concluded that it did not include those who only pretended or feigned to absolve, but did not actually impart absolution. Against this

---

9 Noldin, l. c. N. 371; Genicot, l. c. N. 354; Ferreres, l. c. N. 688; Chelodi, l. c. N. 90; Sole, l. c. p. 353; Capello, l. c. N. 52.

10 Pennachi, l. c. p. 332.

11 S. C. S. O., Jan. 13, 1892.

12 S. C. S. O., June 27, 1866; April 4, 1871.

13 Wernz, Jus Decretalium, T. VI, p. 451; Capello, l. c. p. 54.

interpretation the Sacred Penitentiary decreed that confessors simulating absolution of an accomplice *in peccato turpi* do not escape the excommunication reserved in the constitution *"Sacramentum Poenitentiae"* of Benedict XIV.[14] This declaration of the Sacred Penitentiary was repeated by the Holy Office.[15] However, in order that a priest who pretends to absolve may fall under the excommunication it is necessary for the penitent to be deceived and think himself truly absolved.[16]

If a penitent should fail in good faith to confess the sin of complicity, absolution given by his accomplice would be both valid and licit, and the confessor would not incur the censure.[17] Even if the penitent wilfully held back the sin committed *in materia turpi*, and the priest culpably failed to question him concerning it, nevertheless the confessor would escape the penalty, because absolution was not given from the sin of complicity, and the penitent withheld his sin through no inducement of the priest.[18] This opinion receives confirmation from a response of the Sacred Penitentiary, of May 15, 1877, which reads as follows:

To the question: An incurrat censuras, in absolventes complicem in peccato turpi latas, qui complicem quidem absolvit, sed complicem, qui complicitatis peccatum in confessione non declaravit? (Ratio dubitandi esse videtur, quia talis sacerdos, etiamsi complex sacrilege hujus peccati confessionem omitteret, et ipse culpabiliter ab interrogando abstineret, non tamen absolvit ab hujusmodi complicitatis culpa, utpote non declarata, nec subjecta clavibus.) The Sacred Penitentiary replied: "Privationem jurisdictionis absolvendi complicem in peccato turpi, et adnexam excommunicationem, quatenus confessarius

14 S. Peniten., March 1, 1878.
15 S. C. S. O., Dec. 5, 1883.
16 Capello, l. c. p. 52.
17 Capello, l. c. p. 51.
18 Cavigioli, l. c. N. 75.

illum absolverit, esse in ordine ad ipsum peccatum turpe, in quo idem confessarius complex fuit."

But suppose the penitent held back the sin through undue influence exerted upon him by his accomplice. Here there is question, not of culpable carelessness or negligence in questioning the penitent, but of an active, positive effort which results in concealment of the sin. Benedict XIV did not legislate on this point. It was settled by a declaration of the Holy Office to the effect that the excommunication reserved in the Bull "*Sacramentum Poenitentiae*" is not avoided by a confessor absolving or pretending to absolve his accomplice who, indeed, does not confess the sin of complicity from which he is not yet absolved, if he has so acted, whether in good or bad faith, because the confessor has induced him either directly or indirectly to do this.[19] This declaration has been introduced into the New Law.

A much mooted question is that concerning the power of a priest to absolve his accomplice who has already received direct absolution of the sin *in materia turpi* from another confessor. Some contend that if the sin of complicity alone is confessed to the priest accomplice the absolution would be invalid, and in consequence the penalty incurred.[20] Capello calls this opinion more probable and a safer one to follow. Noldin formerly embraced this view, but in his latest work expresses (*dixerim*) the opposite opinion, that is, that once absolution is given from the sin by a confessor other than the priest accomplice, the prohibition ceases, although out of a sense of decency and reverence for the sacrament the priest should never afterwards hear the confession of his partner in crime.[21] Lega, Chelodi, Genicot and Ayrinhac also

---

19 S. C. S. O., Feb. 19, 1896.

20 Cerato, Censurae Vigentes Ipso Facto, p. 173; Cavigioli, l. c., n. 71; Gury-Ballerini, Comp. Theol. Moral., p. 539; Pennachi, l. c. p. 324.

21 Noldin, l. c. N. 370, 1 b.

favor the licitness of absolution in such a case.[22] Their opinion would seem to be confirmed by the following response of the Holy Office, "That a confessor is free to absolve his accomplice who has previously obtained absolution from the sin of complicity. But the confessor is advised that unless constrained by necessity he should refrain from hearing the confessions of his accomplice who has already secured absolution from the sin in question."[23] However, as Capello observes, this opinion appears contrary to canon 884 which, without making any distinction, declares absolution of an accomplice *in peccato turpi* invalid.

Most authors affirm the licitness of the absolution if, together with the sin *in materia turpi*, other sins also are confessed.[24] This view is upheld by some of those who deny the lawfulness of absolving from the sin of complicity if it is alone offered as *materia libera*. But even in this case Pennachi denies the power of the confessor accomplice to absolve.[25]

In conclusion we would say that inasmuch as there is question of *materia odiosa*, and a real doubt exists, the opinion favoring absolution, even if the sin *contra sextum* be the only one confessed, is at least safe to follow.

A doubt having arisen as to whether the law applied if the sin had been committed before the confessor's ordination to the priesthood, the matter was laid before the Sacred Penitentiary. The response given was that in this case also the confessor would violate the law by granting absolution to his accomplice.[26]

Some uncertainty also prevailed concerning the scope of the *peccatum turpe* of Benedict's law. The matter was settled by the Holy Office in a response in

---

22 Lega, De Delictis et Poenis, P. 6; Chelodi, l. c. N. 90; Genicot, l. c. N. 352; Ayrinhac, l. c. p. 318.

23 S. C. S. O. May 29, 1867.

24 Capello, l. c. N. 47; Cavigioli, l. c. N. 74.

25 Pennachi, l. c. p. 327.

26 S. Peniten., Jan. 22, 1879; Capello, l. c. N. 50.

which it was decreed "comprehendi nedum tactus, verum etiam peccata gravia exterius commissa contra castitatem, etiam illa quae consistunt in meris colloquiis et aspectibus qui complicitatem important."[27] Other questions bearing on this matter are treated in the various manuals of moral theology.

In the New Law canon 2367 contains the more important of the laws and decisions or responses given above. With the exception of the clause "unless the dying person refuses to confess to the other priest," there is no change in the New Code. Hence, the interpretations of canonists made in the Old Law still hold in the New. The canon reads as follows:

Par. 1.

One who absolves or pretends to absolve his accomplice *in peccato turpi* incurs an excommunication most specially reserved to the Apostolic See; he incurs this even at the hour of death if another priest, although not approved for hearing confessions, is able to receive the confession of the dying person without infamy or scandal resulting from his act, unless the dying person refuses to confess to the other priest.

Par. 2.

One who absolves or attempts to absolve his accomplice who does not indeed confess the sin of complicity from which he is not yet absolved, but acts in this way because he was induced to do so directly or indirectly by the confessor, also does not escape the penalty noted in paragraph one.

The only words of the above canon not found in the decrees or decisions previously quoted are, as we observed before, "unless the dying person refuses to confess to the other priest." Formerly it was disputed whether or not in such a case the priest accomplice could give absolution. No authoritative decree had been issued and hence the matter remained doubtful until the Code expressly decided in favor of

---

27 S. C. S. O., May 28, 1873.

the absolution. Capello remarks that an explicit denial on the part of the penitent is not necessary. An implicit refusal, indicated by either words, or a nod, or signs, e. g., if the dying person showed in some manner that he would only unwillingly, or with difficulty, confess to the other priest, would suffice.[28]

In order to incur the penalty there must have been complicity *in peccato turpi,* which supposes a sin against the sixth commandment, grave and external, whatever be its specific nature otherwise, committed by the free, mutual, and externally manifested consent of the two parties, whether of the same or different sex.[29] A mere hearing of the confession of an accomplice is not sufficient. There must be absolution, or simulation of absolution.

Presumption is not required to incur this censure, but inasmuch as it is a medicinal punishment, ignorance that is not crass or supine will excuse from it.[30] Nor would a priest become subject to the penalty if he were under the necessity of not betraying himself because when the sin was committed he was not recognized as a priest.[31] Likewise, if absolution should be imparted through inadvertence, or if the confessor seriously doubted whether the penitent was his accomplice, in both cases the priest would not fall under the excommunication.[32]

To absolve from this censure very special faculties have to be obtained from the Holy See except in cases of urgent necessity or danger of death, as provided in canons 2252 and 2254. Canon 2254, in par. 3, explicitly declares that the recourse stipulated in par. 1 must be imposed when absolution is granted from the sin of complicity in an urgent case, even though on account of peculiar circumstances the recourse be morally impossible.

---

28 Capello, l. c. N. 53.
29 Ayrinhac, l. c. p. 317.
30 Canon 2229, par. 3.
31 Capello, l. c. p. 51; Chelodi, l. c. p. 105.
32 Capello, l. c. p. 51; Chelodi, l. c. p. 105.

CHAPTER VI

THE CRIME OF SOLICITATION

The crime of solicitation in the technical, canonical sense, consists essentially in the making use of the office of confessor to draw others into sin against the sixth commandment.[1]

There are no records extant of penal legislation against this abuse in the early days of the Church. The first punitive measure in this matter was taken by the Council of Treves (a. 1227) which decreed a penalty of deposition and excommunication against "*sacerdotes sollicitantes in confessione feminas ad turpia.*" Pius IV was the second to legislate on the subject. In his constitution "*Cum Sicut*" of April 16, 1561, he promulgated a law against solicitation in Spain. Next, Gregory XV confirmed this local law and extended it to the whole Church in his constitution "*Universi*" of August 30, 1622. He made an important addition to its provisions also by imposing a strict obligation on those solicited of denouncing the guilty confessor. Succeeding pontiffs endeavored to eliminate a certain laxity that had arisen in connection with the penalties already enacted.[2] Among these the most prominent was Benedict XIV who in his constitution "*Sacramentum Poenitentiae*" of June 1, 1741, confirmed and amplified the constitution "Universi" of Gregory XV, authentically interpreted it, and settled many doubts to which it had given rise.[3] This last legislation, after being repeated and confirmed by several decrees of the Sacred Congregation of the Inquisition and the Sacred Congregation of

---

1 Ayrinhac, l. c. p. 319.

2 Alex. VII, Sept. 24, 1665, prop. 6. 7.; Denzinger-Bannwart, Enchirid. n. 1106, sq.

3 Wernz, VI, N. 469.

the Propagation of the Faith,[4] has finally been embodied in the New Code.[5]

Inasmuch as the constitution "*Universi*" of Gregory XV is, as it were, the corner stone of legislation on solicitation, we shall reproduce those parts of it which bear particularly on the matter in hand.

"Ac praeterea ne in futurum de poena his delinquentibus imponenda, et de modo contra eosdem procedendi ab aliquo dubitari possit, statuimus, decernimus, et declaramus, quod omnes, et singuli sacerdotes, tam saeculares, quam quorumvis, etiam quomodolibet exemptorum, ac Sedi Apostolicae immediate subjectorum ordinum, Institutorum, Societatum, et Congregationum Regulares, cujuscumque dignitatis, et praeeminentiae, aut quovis privilegio muniti existant, qui personas, quaecumque illae sint, ad inhonesta, sive inter se, sive cum aliis quomodolibet perpetranda in actu sacramentalis confessionis, sive antea vel post immediate, seu occasione, vel praetextu confessionis hujusmodi, etiam ipsa confessione non secuta, sive extra occasionem confessionis in confessionario, aut in loco quocumque ubi confessiones sacramentales audiantur, seu ad confessionem audiendam electo, simulantes ibidem confessiones audire, sollicitare, vel provocare tentaverint, aut cum eis illicitos, et inhonestos sermones, sive tractatus habuerint, in officio S. Inquisitionis severissime, ut infra puniantur . . . . et quos in aliquo ex hujusmodi nefariis excessibus culpabiles repererint, in eos pro criminum qualitate et circumstantiis, suspensionem ab executione ordinis, privationis beneficiorum, dignitatum, et officiorum quorumcumque, ac perpetuae inhabilitatis ad illa, necnon vocis activae et passivae si regulares fuerint, exilii, damnationis ad triremes, et

---

4 Instr. S. C. S. O., 20 Feb. 1687, 20 July, 1890; S. C. de P. F., In Collec. T. 2, N. 1604; Instr. S. C. S. O., 6 Aug. 1897 in cit. Collec. T. 2, N. 1977.

5 Canon 904.

carceris etiam in perpetuum absque ulla spe gratiae, aliasque poenas decernant, eos quoque si pro delicti enormitate graviores poenas meruerint, debita praecedente degradatione, curiae saeculari puniendos tradant. . . . .

Mandantes omnibus confessariis, ut suos poenitentes, quos noverint fuisse ab aliis ut supra sollicitatos, moneant de obligatione denuntiandi sollicitantes, seu ut praefertur tractantes, Inquisitoribus seu locorum Ordinariis praedictis. Quodsi hoc officium praetermiserint, vel poenitentes docuerint non teneri ad denuntiandum confessarios sollicitantes, seu tractantes, ut supra, iidem locorum Ordinarii, et Inquisitores illos pro modo culpae punire non negligant."

Benedict XIV in his constitution "*Sacramentum Poenitentiae*" confirmed Gregory's "*Universi,*" and also made several important additions. The manner or method of solicitation was more clearly defined: "*Ad inhonesta et turpia sollicitare vel provocare, sive verbis, sive signis, sive nutibus, sive tactu, sive per scripturam, aut tunc, aut post legendam, tentaverint.*" Furthermore, he inserted the words "*temerario ausu*" in the clause pertaining to illicit conversations: "*Aut cum eis illicitos et inhonestos sermones, vel tractatus temerario ausu habuerint.*" Also, in regard to the obligation of a penitent to denounce a priest guilty of solicitation, it was stated that the obligation should be imposed "*etiamsi sacerdos sit, qui jurisdictione ad absolutionem valide impertiendam careat, aut sollicitatio inter confessarium et poenitentem mutua fuerit, sive sollicitationi poenitens consenserit, sive consensum minime praestiterit, vel longum tempus post ipsam sollicitationem jam effluxerit, aut sollicitatio a confessario, non pro se ipso, sed pro alia persona, peracta fuerit.*" Moreover, a sanction was enacted against those who refused to comply with the command of a confessor to denounce a guilty priest: "*Caveant insuper diligenter confesarii ne poenitenti-*

bus, quos noverint ab alio sollicitatos, sacramentalem absolutionem impertiant, nisi prius denuntiationem praedictam ad effectum perducentes, delinquentem indicaverint competenti judici, vel saltem se, cum primum poterunt, delaturos spondeant, ac promittant."

Previously, on March 10, 1677, the Holy Office had decreed that all the faithful were obliged under pain of excommunication *latae sententiae* to denounce confessors who abused the sacrament of penance to solicit their penitents. But since the Benedictine law failed to designate any others than the person solicited, the latter only would now incur the penalty.

Pius IX in his "*Apostolicae Sedis*" made no change in the punishment against those who solicited, but in respect to the one subject to solicitation it was enacted that the following incurred an excommunication *latae sententiae* reserved to no one: Negligentes sive culpabiliter omittentes denuntiare infra mensem confessarios, sive sacerdotes a quibus sollicitati fuerint ad turpia in quibuslibet casibus expressis a praedecessoribus Nostris Greg. XIV, Const. "*Universi*" 10 Aug. 1611, et Bened. XIV, Const. "*Sacramentum Poenitentiae*" 1 June, 1741. By this legislation an unreserved *latae sententiae* excommunication was imposed, but confessors received no admonition or precept to withhold absolution in case denunciation was not made or promised.

Finally, the New Code decrees that he who has committed the crime of solicitation, as set forth in canon 904, should be suspended from the celebration of Mass and from hearing sacramental confessions, or even, according to the gravity of the offence, declared ineligible to hear them, should be deprived of all benefices, dignities, right to vote or to be voted for, and declared unable to acquire again these privileges. In particularly grave cases he is subject to degradation.

Moreover, any one of the faithful who within a month knowingly fails to denounce him by whom he was solicited, in opposition to the provisions of canon 904, incurs an unreserved *latae sententiae* excommunication, nor is he to be absolved until he has satisfied the obligation, or seriously promised that he will fulfill it.[6]

In canon 904 we read "According to the norm of the Apostolic Constitutions, and especially of the constitution "*Sacramentum Poenitentiae*" of Benedict XIV, June 1, 1741, a penitent must within a month denounce a priest guilty of the crime of solicitation in confession to the Ordinary of the place or the Sacred Congregation of the Holy Office; and the confessor is bound by a grave obligation (*graviter onerata ejus conscientia*) to inform the penitent of this duty.

Obligation of Denunciation

In discussing canon 2368 we shall treat first of the second paragraph, viz: that concerning the obligation of denouncing a priest who solicits. For in so doing we shall necessarily explain much that pertains to the first paragraph.

"*Fidelis*" signifies both male and female, and is to be taken generally as comprehending all the faithful. *Impuberes,* however, are not subject to the penalty. For by virtue of canon 2230 they are excused from punishments *latae sententiae.* But the obligation of denunciation remains, and can be enforced *sub poena censurae* once the age of puberty, which is the fourteenth year completed for males and the twelfth year completed for females, is attained.[7]

Cerato limits the law to those belonging to the Latin Church. But since canon 904 rules according to the Apostolic Constitutions relating to this matter, the Greeks also must be included. For the constitution "*Etsi Pastoralis*" of Benedict XIV declared Latins

---

6 Canon 2368.

7 Cerato, l. c. N. 67.

and Greeks equally subject to the laws against solicitation.[8]

While a strict obligation of disclosure to the proper authorities would bind others beside the solicited party who should obtain certain knowledge of the solicitation, unless the crime were revealed to them in order to obtain their advice,[9] yet should they refuse or fail to make the denunciation, no censure would be incurred. For only the victim of solicitation is bound under penalty of excommunication to denounce. This is evident from the words, "*eum, a quo sollicitatus fuerit.*"

Who should be denounced? Any priest guilty of solicitation while he acts as confessor, even if he lacked jurisdiction to hear confessions. Hence the law does not comprehend lay persons, or clerics in minor orders, or deacons or sub-deacons, although these also by reason of natural law should be reported. It is disputed whether or not bishops are likewise subject to denunciation. Cerato thinks they are included by reason of the words "*cujuscumque dignitatis et praeeminentiae, aut quovis privilegio et indulto munitos*" of the constitution "*Sacramentum Poenitentiae.*"[10] Farrugia states that according to the New Law they must be denounced because by virtue of canon 2227, par. 2, bishops are not exempt from censures *latae sententiae* (of excommunication).[11] This reason, however, is of no avail. For there is no question in the case under discussion of a bishop incurring a censure *latae sententiae* of excommunication. Rather, it is the penitent who might contract the censure. Vermeersch is of the opinion that probably bishops are excluded because they are not subject to the inquisitors.[12] But against this view are the words of Benedict XIV above cited "*aut quovis*

8 May 26, 1742.
9 S. C. S. O., March 10, 1677.
10 Cerato, l. c. N. 67.
11 Farrugia, l. c. p. 28.
12 Vermeersch, l. c. N. 187.

privilegio aut indulto munitos." Accordingly, Cerato's opinion seems more probable.

What must be said if the confessor does not himself solicit, but merely consents to solicitation made by a penitent? According to Capello, it is controverted whether or not in this case denunciation must follow. Furthermore, he himself thinks the controversy is not without solid basis because the law speaks explicitly *de confessario sollicitante only.*[13] But this reason is faulty. For canon 904 expressly declares the obligation of denunciation as posited in accordance with the Apostolic Constitutions, and particularly with the constitution "*Sacramentum Poenitentiae*" of Benedict XIV. Now, this latter constitution embraces not only those priests who solicit but also those who "*cum eis* (*poenitentibus*) *illicitos et inhonestos sermones, vel tractatus temerario ausu habuerint.*" Hence, even though a priest does not himself solicit, but only consents to the solicitation of a penitent, nevertheless, as D'Annibale points out, "*palam est in rem turpem eum convenire; atqui hoc est inhonestos tractatus habere.*"[14] This opinion receives confirmation from a decree of the Holy Office. To the question, "Whether a confessor who consents to solicitation, but immediately ceases to speak further *de illa turpi materia* by reason of postponing completion of the crime to another time, and who does not impart absolution to his penitent, incurs the penalties contained in the Bull of Gregory, and should be denounced?" it was answered, "The confessor does incur the penalty and must be denounced, the probable opinion to the contrary being rejected."[15] However, should a priest through grave fear consent to a penitent's solicitation he could not then legitimately be denounced. For on account of this grave fear the *inhonesti tractatus* would not arise

13 Capello, l. c. N. 142.
14 D'Annibale, Summa Theol. Moralis, Pars. 3, N. 365.
15 S. C. S. O., Feb. 11, 1661.

temerario ausu on the confessor's part, as is required by Benedict's constitution.

By the phrase "*praetextu confessionis*" is meant a pretext on the confessor's part. Accordingly, if a penitent feigns confession in order that he may solicit a confessor there is no *praetextus confessionis.*[16] St. Alphonsus seems to go too far when he says that if both confessor and penitent from mutual agreement pretend confession, *praetextus confessionis* is not verified.[17] Vermeersch observes that this opinion lacks weight and can be admitted only by reason of its extrinsic probability.[18]

Further information regarding *praetextus confessionis* and other moral aspects of solicitation can be obtained from the various moral theologians.

The obligation of denunciation remains even if a long time has elapsed since the crime was committed, if the offence cannot be juridically proved, or if the guilty priest previously had been denounced and punished for a similar delinquency. But if the penitent had solicited and the priest only given consent, *per accidens* denunciation would not have to follow should the penitent in his disclosure necessarily have to manifest his own sin.[19]

Authors generally maintain that the amendment of a guilty confessor does not excuse his penitent from the obligation of reporting him.[20] Their opinion is based upon the theory that the primary purpose of this law is not amendment of the offender but rather security of souls and reverence for the sacrament of penance to be obtained through certain punishment of this detestable crime. Others think that if many years have elapsed since the offence was committed, and moral certainty of the priest's

---

16 Vermeersch, l. c. N. 190, 4.

17 St. Alphonsus, Theol. Moral. VI, 679.

18 Vermeersch, l. c. N. 190, 3.

19 Genicot, l. c. N. 395.

20 Cerato, l. c. N. 67; Chelodi, l. c. N. 91; Ferreres, l. c. N. 694; Noldin, l. c. N. 376.

complete amendment is had, probably denunciation is no longer obligatory.[21] The first opinion is more common and seems more in conformity with the spirit of the law.

In order that a penitent may incur the penalty for failure to denounce a guilty confessor full knowledge and deliberation are required. This follows from the use of "*scienter*" which, according to canon 2229, par. 1, signifies that any diminution of imputability whatsoever, whether on the part of the intellect or the will, excuses from *latae sententiae* punishments. Wherefore, even crass ignorance will exempt one from contracting the censure. However, it does not also take away the obligation. This will have to be fulfilled under penalty of the censure once it is clearly known. Moreover, it would seem that now grave fear will excuse in all cases. In this connection Capello states that *per se* grave fear of loss of life, good name, or fortune, whether to one's self or relatives, removes the obligation of denouncing. But if the solicitation occasions public scandal or common harm, private inconvenience never frees from the obligation.[22] Cerato, on the other hand, thinks that by virtue of canon 2229 even if public scandal or loss should result from a refusal to make known a guilty priest, nevertheless, grave fear will exempt one from the censure, and hence also implicitly from the obligation as long as the fear lasts.[23] This opinion can certainly be drawn from the wording of canon 2229. In paragraph one, quoted above, which contains *praesumpserit, etc.*, no qualification as to public loss is found. It is only when a canon does not employ such words as *praesumpserit, etc.*, as paragraph two states, that grave fear will not excuse from *latae sententiae* penalties if the *delictum* brings contempt upon the faith or ecclesiastical authority, or results in public loss of

21 Genicot, l. c. N. 397.
22 Capello, l. c. N. 142; Genicot, l. c. N. 397; Noldin, l. c. N. 379.
23 Cerato, l. c. N. 67.

souls. It follows, therefore, that when the law does use such words as *praesumpserit, scienter,* etc., it makes no difference in regard to the penalty whether or not the crime causes a public loss of souls. It would seem, however, that in such a case the obligation to denounce would still exist *ex jure naturali.*

The denunciation must be made within a month from the time one learns of his obligation, the excommunication attached, and the time allowed in which to fulfill it.[24] The time is *utile.*[25]

A confessor is obliged *sub gravi* to instruct a penitent who has been solicited concerning his duty.[26] He must do this even though the penitent is in good faith and it is foreseen that he will not carry out the mandate. In urgent danger of death, however, his obligation to do this ceases if it is feared that the monition will jeopardize the penitent's eternal salvation.[27] The instruction must not be given if the person solicited should in his innocence not understand the significance of solicitation. But if he discovered its meaning later he would have to be informed what the law requires. Some theologians think that probably a confessor may not be constrained to admonish a penitent to denounce under the following conditions taken conjointly:

1. Provided no loss or harm will result to souls from omitting the denunciation. This condition would be verified if the guilty confessor should become hopelessly deaf so that he could no longer hear confessions.

2. If the penitent will not *hic et nunc* fulfill his obligation, and there is no likelihood of his doing so in the future on account of special circumstances that *per se* will indefinitely continue to exist.[28]

In case a person refuses to make the necessary denunciation he is not to receive absolution until either

---

24 Capello, l. c. N. 141.
25 Lega, l. c. p. 8.
26 Canon 904.
27 Vermeersch, l. c. N. 193; Capello, p. 137, footnote 2.
28 Capello, l. c. p. 137, footnote 2; Noldin, l. c. N. 378 1 b.

he has satisfied his obligation, or at least seriously promised to do so. It should be noticed that the censure incurred is unreserved, and that, therefore, any confessor may absolve from it if the penitent makes a promise to observe the law. Furthermore, should the penitent promise to denounce, but afterwards without any justifying cause fail to keep his word, he would not again contract a censure, although he would commit a grave sin. The reason is because the Code makes no mention of reincidence. Nevertheless, the obligation to denounce would remain, and the confessor could refuse to impart absolution until it had been fulfilled.[29]

Penalties

In regard to the penalties against priests who are found guilty of solicitation, it is to be observed that in the New Law as well as in the Old they are all *ferendae sententiae.* Degradation is designated in the New Law, as in the old, as one of the punishments to be inflicted in cases of a grave nature. But this penalty should rarely be applied. For according to a decree of the Holy Office Gregory XV ordained this punishment rather to inspire fear than to have it carried into effect.[30]

---

29 Cerato, l. c. N. 67 2 d.
30 20 Feb. 1867.

CHAPTER VII

VIOLATION OF THE SEAL OF CONFESSION

The Church has always firmly maintained and defended the inviolability of the seal of confession. She knows that in a matter so delicate only the most scrupulous care to avoid even the shadow of a suspicion against her of remissness or condonation of a deliberate or culpable offence against the sacramental seal, only the most rigid insistence on absolute fidelity on the part of her confessors to this fundamentally necessary law, could inspire that confidence in the faithful which they need in order to satisfy completely the divine obligation of confessing their sins to a priest. Hence, she decrees very severe penalties against infractions of this law. However, it is not to be inferred from this that instances of such offences have been or are frequent. For in this case gravity of the punishment is not to be measured by the prevalence of an abuse, but rather both by the very nature of the object of the law and the fact that enemies of the Church and others have at times denied its absolute binding force in the civil courts, and attempted to compel her ministers to divulge as evidence what they have learned in the confessional. Her severe sanctions for this law serve, as it were, as a protest against these unholy endeavors to interfere in this divinely sealed confidence.

General Principles

The obligation of keeping secret a sacramental confession arises from natural, and ecclesiastical law. It prohibits the confessor from speaking outside of confession of those matters learned from the penitent's confession. Not even with the penitent himself may the priest speak unless he first receives his permission. The obligation comes only from a sacramental confession, that is, one made with the purpose of obtaining absolution. It binds principally the confessor, and secondarily all others to whom knowledge of the subject of the seal has in any manner come, e. g., an interpreter employed by a person to help him make his confession; bystanders who accidentally or on purpose have heard something pertaining to confession; likewise all those to whom they may impart this knowledge; all those to whom a confessor sacrilegiously or imprudently discloses confessional secrets; superiors from whom either by the confessor or the penitent power of absolving from reserved sins has been asked.

The seal may be violated directly or indirectly. A direct violation takes place if both a sin told in confession and the person of the penitent who confessed the sin are revealed.

An indirect violation occurs if from what the confessor says or does there is real danger that the sin of the penitent may become known, or confession rendered odious.[1]

Penalties

In the early years of the Church there is no evidence of penalties for a violation of the seal. The first record of a punishment for this crime is that enacted by the synod of Dovin in Armenia A. D. 527-531,[2] according to which priests guilty of this offence should be punished with an anathema. In Gratian's decretals we find deposition noted as a penalty for violating the seal.[3] Finally the Fourth

---

1 Noldin, l. c. p. 473, et seq. (1920).

2 Canon 20 in Hefele, History of the Councils, Vol. IV.

3 C 2 D VI "Si hoc fecerit, deponatur et omnibus diebus vitae suae ignominiosus peregrinando pergat."

Council of the Lateran (1215) in canon 21 decreed deposition and perpetual confinement in a monastery for this offence. These penalties were repeated by the Council of Treves in 1227.[4] However, due to interference on the part of the civil authorities the sentence of perpetual imprisonment in a monastery could not always be enforced, and so in course of time this punishment underwent some modifications.

Before the new Code, according to Wernz after he had reviewed the above punishments, a priest guilty of presumptuously divulging a sin learned from sacramental confession to a third person distinct from the penitent was to be punished by a penalty *ferendae sententiae* of deposition from the priestly office. But inasmuch as perpetual confinement in a monastery which, according to the decretals should have been added to this deposition, often by reason of the unjust laws of the State forbidding the Church to impose temporal punishment, could not be inflicted, its place was taken by a voluntary withdrawal to a house for delinquent clerics, or a monastery of strict discipline. But if the violator of the seal were not a priest confessor, but any other cleric, or a lay person who revealed a sin known from confession, or if not a sin, some defect whose disclosure was a hardship to the penitent, or if the confessor should make mention of a sin, not, however, to a third person, but to the penitent himself, or if he should not break the seal presumptuously, then in these cases, the ordinary penalties enacted by law for a violation of the seal were not to be applied, but other extraordinary ones should be inflicted according to the prudent estimation of the judge who was to be guided in his decision by the quality of the offence.[5]

In the New Law, according to canon 2369, par. 1, a confessor who presumes to violate the sacramental *sigillum* directly incurs an excommunication reserved

4 Mansi, Coll. Conc. Vol. 23.
5 Wernz, VI, p. 444, et seq.

in a very special manner to the Apostolic See (this penalty is *latae sententiae*); but one who only indirectly breaks the seal becomes subject to the penalties enumerated in canon 2368, par. 1 against those guilty of the crime of solicitation, viz: he should be suspended from celebrating Mass and from hearing sacramental confessions, and if the gravity of the offence warrants it, he may even be declared unable to exercise the functions of confessor; he should be deprived of all benefices, dignities, active and passive vote (right to vote and be voted for), and declared unable to acquire these privileges again, and in the more serious cases he should be degraded. (These penalties are, of course, *ferendae sententiae.*)

Par. 2 states that all those who rashly (*temere*) violate the provisions of canon 889, par. 2, which asserts that interpreters, and all others to whom in any manner confessional knowledge has come, are also obliged to keep the seal, according to the gravity of their guilt should be punished with a suitable penalty, which may even be excommunication. (This penalty, likewise, is *ferendae sententiae.*)

In comparing this canon with the Old Law it is to be noted first that the penalty for a direct presumptuous violation of the secret is now milder than before. It is true that the penalty now is *latae sententiae,* whereas before it was *ferendae sententiae.* But, nevertheless, deposition once inflicted is a more severe punishment than excommunication, even though most specially reserved. This fact is shown from a consideration of canon 2314, pars. 1 and 2. In par. 1 of this canon it is stated that all formal apostates, heretics and schismatics incur *ipso facto* an excommunication. But in par. 2 we read that these same offenders if, after a warning, they do not repent, should be deprived of any benefice, dignity, pension, office, or other function they may have in the Church, be declared *infames,* and clerics after a second admonition should be *deposed.*

In the Old Law the punishment for a presumptuous indirect violation by a confessor seems to have been the same as that enacted for a direct violation. Wernz makes no distinction between a direct and an indirect presumptuous disclosure to a third party distinct from the penitent. The new law, however, has two separate penalties. Those for the indirect revelation, which we enumerated above, are *ferendae sententiae,* as in the Old Law.

One exception to this might be found in the case in which a priest speaks about confessional matter to the penitent himself. Canonists generally consider this an indirect violation of the seal, and so for this one case there was an extraordinary penalty *ferendae sententiae* distinct from that decreed against other presumptuous disclosures of the confessional secret by a priest confessor.

There is no difference in the Old and New Law between the penalties decreed against those other than confessors to whom knowledge of confessional matter in any way comes, for now, as formerly, the imposition of a punishment is left to the prudent discretion of the judge. The New Law, however, explicitly mentions that the punishment may be excommunication.

In the New Law there is no specific penalty for non-presumptuous violation of the seal by a priest confessor. This offence was classed among those left to the prudence of the judge to punish.

A confessor may contract the penalties of this canon even though he should hear without jurisdiction the confession which he discloses.[6] But they would not be incurred by a lay person, not even if he pretended that he was a priest and heard the confessions of the faithful who came to him in good faith.[7]

An indirect violation is one special to confessors. It would be considered an indirect violation if a

---

6 Chelodi, l. c. p. 107.

7 Chelodi, l. c.; Schmalzgrueber, Lib. V Pars. II Tit. XXXVIII N. 80.

confessor should speak without permission of some sin learned in the confessional to the penitent himself.[8]

Par. 2 of this canon comprehends interpreters, theologians, superiors, and all others who by chance, or deliberately, or in any other manner have learned something protected by the sacramental seal.

Inasmuch as the penalty of excommunication for a direct violation is *latae sententiae,* and presumption is required in order to incur it, any diminution of imputability, whether on the part of the intellect or will, will excuse from it.[9] This is not the case with the other penalties stated for an indirect violation, or against those who violate canon 889, par. 2, because they are *ferendae sententiae.*

---

8 Chelodi, l. c.
9 Canon 2229, par. 2.

CHAPTER VIII

CONSECRATION OF A BISHOP WITHOUT THE APOSTOLIC MANDATE

In Decretal Law Metropolitans were accorded the privilege of consecrating suffragan bishops.[1] But later when the conferring of cathedral churches was reserved to the Roman Pontiff, the consecration of bishops as a natural consequence also became reserved to the same person. Abuses on the part of certain Metropolitans also helped to bring about this reservation.[2] In his letter *"In Postremo"* of Oct. 20, 1756, Benedict XIV concedes that in former times Metropolitans had the right to consecrate suffragan bishops, but that now the consecration must be done either by the Roman Pontiff himself or by one expressly delegated by the pontiff for that purpose. Later, Pius VI in his encyclical *"Charitas"* of April 13, 1791, enacted several penalties against violators of this reservation. Offences committed by French bishops gave rise to these severe sanctions. Those guilty of consecrating without a pontifical mandate, and also those who assisted at the consecration, were suspended from all exercise of the episcopal order. Moreover, all who helped in the consecration by advice, consent, or other aid, were declared suspended from the exercise of the sacerdotal or any other order which they might have. Furthermore, bishops who were thus illicitly consecrated should not dare, under pain of the same suspension, to arrogate to themselves episcopal jurisdiction, or any other authority over souls, which they had never received, or to give dimissorial letters, to constitute pastors, vicars,

---

1 C. 6, X de temporibus ordinationum et qualitate ordinandorum, I, II.

2 Gasparri, De Sacra Ordinatione II, N. 795.

missionaries, etc. And if they dared to make any appointments, such appointments were declared null and void. Also, neither the one who consecrated nor the one consecrated should venture under penalty of suspension to confirm illicitly, or to confer orders, or to exercise in any way the episcopal order from which he was suspended. And if any received orders from these suspended bishops, they, too, would be suspended. Moreover, if these latter exercised the orders thus illicitly obtained they would incur an irregularity.

The reservation above cited finds expression in the Roman Pontifical. In the title "*De Consecratione electi in episcopum*" we read as follows:

"Nemo consecrari debet, nisi prius constet consecratori de commissione consecrandi, sive per Litteras Apostolicas, si sit extra Curiam, sive per commissionem vivae vocis oraculo, a Summo Pontifice consecratori factam, si consecrator ipse sit Cardinalis."

In the New Law it is stated that episcopal consecration is reserved to the Roman Pontiff in such a manner that no bishop is permitted to consecrate a person bishop unless he is certain of the papal mandate.[3]

As noted above, this mandate is given orally if the consecration is performed by a Cardinal (who, it may be supposed, resides in Rome), but if it occurs outside the *Curia,* the consecrator needs an Apostolic Letter before he is allowed to perform the function. It should be observed, however, that the law does not require actual possession of this mandate. Certain knowledge of the execution or dispatch of the letter will suffice if this knowledge is received from an *official* source.[4] But if the information were unofficially forwarded, even though it were certainly reliable, it would not avail to permit the consecration before actual arrival of the mandate. Thus, e. g., the bishop-elect of the State of Assumption in the West

3 Canon 953.
4 Canon 53.

Indies was consecrated by another bishop "*non praesentatis Litteris Apostolicis provisionis et praefectionis suae in Episcopum ejusdem Ecclesiae, quae tamen revera concessae prius et expeditae fuerant, deque ipsa concessione et expeditione praeviis quibusdam informationibus aliqualiter constabat.*" To the doubt proposed whether or not this consecration was valid, it was answered: "The consecration of the bishop . . . . as far as the sacrament and impression of the character are concerned was valid; but in respect to the licit execution of the order, it was null and void, and both the bishop so consecrated and the one who consecrated require absolution and dispensation."[5]

On the other hand, a doubt was proposed to the Sacred Congregation of the Propagation of the Faith concerning the consecration of the bishop-elect of Pekin who was consecrated before reception of the Apostolic Letters. The reasons adduced for proceeding before arrival of the letters were first, because the consecration could no longer be deferred, and secondly, because certain and *authentic* knowledge was had of the dispatch of these letters. This consecration was declared licit.[6]

Certain and authentic knowledge could be obtained in this matter if a message were sent by the *Cardinalis Cancellarius Sanctae Romanae Ecclesiae*[7] by telephone, telegraph, or even wireless, to the effect that the Apostolic Letters had been expedited.

Should a bishop be consecrated without the apostolic mandate in violation of canon 953, the consecrating bishop, the assisting bishops or priests who assist in the place of bishops, and the prelate consecrated are *ipso facto* suspended. The suspension is to last until the Apostolic See grants a dispensation.

---

5 Alex. VII, Litt. Ap. "Alias," 27 Feb. 1660.
6 Collectanea S. C. Prop. de Fide, N. 551.
7 Canon 260.

"Bishop" in this canon signifies either a residential or a titular bishop. Cardinals, however, are not included because they are not expressly mentioned.[8] Nor does the law affect oriental bishops. For in addition to the prescription of canon 1 of the New Code, episcopal consecration in the Oriental Church is not reserved to the Roman Pontiff. In this Church the Metropolitan, or a bishop delegated by him, consecrates suffragans, and the Patriarch, or a bishop delegated by him, consecrates Metropolitans.[9] But the law would bind a Latin prelate who should illicitly receive consecration from a member of the Oriental Church.[10]

The suspension is a general one. Hence it embraces all the effects of a suspension from both office and benefice.[11]

Finally, the suspension is not a censure, but a vindictive punishment. For its cessation does not depend on amendment of the culprit, but on the will of the Apostolic See.[12]

---

8 Canon 2227, par. 2.
9 Gasparri, l. c. N. 797.
10 Capello, l. c. N. 165.
11 Canon 2278.
12 Canon 2286.

CHAPTER IX

SIMONY IN THE ADMINISTRATION OR RECEPTION OF THE SACRAMENTS

Scarcely any evidence of simony can be found in the records of the early years of Christianity. The fierce persecutions offered no incentive to simoniacal practices. But about the fourth century conditions changed. With official recognition of the Church came also a relaxation of the fervor that so characterized the primitive Christians. The temporal wealth of the Church rapidly increased and became an object of desire to lax and tepid Christians. The Arian heresy also helped to weaken ecclesiastical discipline.

In order to defend herself against this deadly evil the Church had to resort to punitive measures. The Council of Chalcedon in 451 enacted the first law against simoniacal ordinations.[1] Other councils and synods soon after enacted similar legislation. The second Synod of Orleans (A. D. 533) declared that if any one obtained the priesthood for money he should be deposed.[2] The sixth Synod of Toledo (A. D. 638) decreed a penalty of excommunication against those who through simony receive consecration. Moreover, both the consecrator and the consecrated should suffer confiscation of their property.[3]

From this multiplied legislation it can easily be deduced that simony was extensively practiced about this time. Many pontiffs attempted to check the evil,

---

1 "If a bishop confers ordination for money and turns the grace which cannot be bought into merchandise, and consecrates a bishop, chorepiscopus, or priest, or deacon, or any other cleric . . . . for the sake of bare gain, upon conviction he shall endanger his own office, and he who is ordained shall have no advantage from his ordination or office obtained by purchase, but shall lose the dignity or post which he has secured for money." Hefele, l. c. 111, p. 386.

2 Hefele, l. c. IV p. 186.

3 Hefele, l. c. IV p. 461.

but it had grown to such proportions in the eleventh century that even the heroic efforts of the great Hildebrand could not completely eradicate it. In a synod held at Rome in 1074 Hildebrand revived all the old decrees against simony. Also in the following year, in a second synod held at Rome, the bishops Sicmar of Bremen, Werner of Strassburg, and others who were guilty of simony, were interdicted from the performance of their functions.[4]

Much of the legislation so far enacted against simony was incorporated in the *Corpus Juris Canonici.* For example, in the *Extravagantes Communes* we read the following taken from a decree of Pope Paul 11:

"All sentences of excommunication, suspension, privation, and interdict, censures and penalties already enacted by preceding pontiffs are confirmed. These punishments are to affect all without exception, even cardinals, patriarchs, bishops, kings and queens. Furthermore, all who have been simoniacally elected are suspended from the execution of their orders. Moreover, all who in any way by giving or receiving have committed simony, or have acted as mediators in this crime, incur an excommunication from which no one except the Roman Pontiff can absolve them, unless they are in danger of death. Finally, any who have knowledge of such a crime are bound by virtue of sacred obedience to reveal the offenders, and if they fail or refuse to make this disclosure they are not to be absolved until they do so."[5]

The Council of Trent confirmed and set forth more clearly the decrees of several popes and councils in this matter. All *ipso facto* penalties hitherto decreed were approved and renewed.[6]

On the promulgation of the "*Apostolicae Sedis,*" according to Gasparri, all the *latae sententiae* penalties previously enacted against simony, since no

---

4 Birkhaeuser, History of the Church, P. 358.
5 C 2 de simonia VI in Extrav. Com.
6 Sess. XXI, Cap. I, de ref.

mention was made of them in this constitution, ceased to exist. The "Apostolicae Sedis" did, indeed, declare that all whom the Council of Trent decreed to be *ipso jure* suspended or interdicted should be still subject to suspension or interdict. But this was true only of censures directly enacted by the council, and not of those merely indirectly decreed in confirming previous legislation, as was the case with the censures under discussion. Hence, those who made or received illegitimate payments by reason of promotion to some grade of the sacred hierarchy committed a sin, and *pro modo culpae* could and should have been punished by their lawful superiors, but they did not incur the *ipso facto* penalties above cited.[7] Wernz admits the abolition of the *latae sententiae* penalties, but observes also that certain *ferendae sententiae* punishments still remained.[8]

In the New Law all persons, even those elevated to the episcopal dignity, who through simony have knowingly ordained any one, or themselves have been advanced to orders, or have administered or received simoniacally other sacraments, are suspected of heresy; clerics, moreover, incur a suspension reserved to the Apostolic See.[9]

As can readily be perceived from a comparison of this canon with the penalties in force before the "*Apostolicae Sedis,*" the present punishments are much milder than those formerly existing. This is due mainly to the fact that abuses are not now as prevalent as in the past. In the New Discipline there is no excommunication either for those who illicitly ordain, or for those who fraudulently receive ordination.

---

7 Gasparri, l. c. N. 1126.

8 Wernz, VI N. 77.

9 Canon 2371.

General Notions of Simony

Before discussing these penalties it will be helpful to set forth some general notions of simony.

There are two main divisions of simony, viz., simony of natural or divine law, and simony of ecclesiastical law. The first is intrinsically evil, but the second becomes wrong only through prohibition of the Church.

Simony of divine law is the deliberate will of buying or selling for a temporal price a thing intrinsically spiritual, e. g., the sacraments, ecclesiastical jurisdiction, consecration, indulgences, etc.; or a temporal thing so connected with a spiritual object that the former can in no way exist without the latter, e. g., an ecclesiastical benefice, etc.; or finally a temporal thing connected with a spiritual, when the spiritual is the object, although only partial, of the contract, e. g., the consecration in the sale of a consecrated chalice.

Simony of ecclesiastical law consists in giving temporal objects annexed to spiritual ones for other temporals attached to spirituals, or spirituals for spirituals, or even temporals for temporals, if this is forbidden by the Church on account of danger of irreverence towards spiritual objects.[10]

Canonists also divide simony into merely internal and external. The former is simply an intention to commit simony, which, however, does not result in an external act; the latter, as its name indicates, is this intention manifested by an outward act.

External simony is called mental if it exists without any agreement, either tacit or expressed, and conventional, if it is accompanied by an expressed or tacit pact.

---

10 Canon 727.

Conventional simony is divided into pure, in which no delivery of price or object is made by either party; into mixed, if one of the two parties delivers either price or object; and into real, in which the simony is consummated by each party through delivery of both price and object.[11]

Other divisions of simony which respect ecclesiastical benefices, as they do not bear on the matter in hand, will not receive consideration.

Penalties

The first part of canon 2371 concerns both clerics and lay persons. Lay persons who illicitly induce a cleric to confer some sacrament upon them are suspected of heresy. They might also incur this suspicion in another way. According to the decretal above quoted,[12] mediators also became subject to an excommunication. Now while mediators are not expressly designated in canon 2371, yet by virtue of canon 2231 both mediators and other co-operators under certain conditions specified in canon 2209 could also contract the penalty. One of the conditions requires necessary cooperation or assistance. Hence, if a lay person rendered indispensable assistance, e. g. in the conferring of orders upon an unworthy candidate, he would be suspected of heresy.

What this suspicion signifies is derived from canon 2315. One suspected of heresy, who, after a warning, does not remove the cause of suspicion is prohibited from exercising the legitimate acts. A cleric should receive a second warning, and if this proves fruitless, he should be suspended *a divinis*. If at the end of six months from the time the penalty was contracted one suspected of heresy has not amended

---

11 Wernz, VI N. 341.
12 C 2 de simonia VI in Extrav. Com.

his course, he is to be considered a heretic subject to the punishment of heretics.[13]

The second penalty is decreed for clerics only. According to Augustine bishops also are included in the word "*clerici.*" He says, "There seems to be little doubt that they are. Canon 2227, par. 2, cannot be quoted against this view, as bishops are especially mentioned at the very beginning of this canon, and moreover, the Council of Trent subjected bishops to all the penalties inflicted by law, and the papal constitutions subjected them to the censure here mentioned. Lastly, it must be remembered that bishops are the ministers of orders. There would be no justice, since simony requires an accomplice, if the greater culprit were less punishable than the simple cleric. The bishops, therefore, according to our view, are also subject to this suspension, which is a general one."[14]

However, the opposite opinion seems to be the true one. The reasons above adduced are not convincing. Cardinals also were expressly designated in the Corpus Juris as being subject to simoniacal punishments, yet by virtue of canon 2227, par. 2, they are not included in the present canon. It is true, too, that bishops are expressly mentioned in the very beginning of the canon, but that is for a different penalty, suspicion of heresy. Hence, it would appear that canon 2227, par. 2, could find application in this case. This is the opinion of Capello, Chelodi, Cerato, Cavigioli, and Ayrinhac.[15]

"*Ordines*" comprehends both major and minor orders, and also, according to canon 950, tonsure.[16]

In order that the penalty may be incurred the simony must be either real or mixed, that is, there must be, first, some kind of a pact or contract. This

---

13 Canon 2315.

14 Augustine, A Commentary on Canon Law, VIII, p. 447.

15 Capello, l. c. N. 166; Chelodi, l. c. N. 93; Cerato, l. c. N. 127; Cavigioli, l. c. N. 186; Ayrinhac, l. c. N. 340.

16 Cerato, l. c. N. 127.

pact is to be understood in a wide sense as signifying any onerous contract whatsoever.[17] And secondly, at least the order or the sacrament must have been conferred,[18] even though the price agreed upon was not paid, and perhaps never will be paid.[19]

The price in a simoniacal contract includes not only money but also all temporal objects on which a price can be set, and which yield temporal advantage. In this wider sense price is designated *munus,* not gratuitous, but one due from a contract, or by virtue of commutative justice.

A threefold kind of *munus* is distinguished:

(1) *Munus a manu,* by which is understood any temporal object on which a price can be set, whether this object be movable or immovable, corporal or incorporeal.

(2) *Munus ab obsequio,* which signifies service of any kind rendered with the understanding that a spiritual favor will be conferred in return.

(3) *Munus a lingua,* which is had if one through an agreement praises or commends a person to another in order to obtain for him some spiritual advantage by way of compensation.[20]

It should be noted that simony is not committed if a temporal thing is given, not for a spiritual object, but on the occasion of it from a just title recognized either by the canons of the Code or custom.[21] In respect to the sacraments the New Law rules that for their administration the minister may not exact or demand anything for any cause whatsoever, either on the occasion of them, or directly or indirectly, with the exception of those offerings prescribed in canon 1507.[22] According to canon 1507, "The prescriptions

---

17 Vermeersch, l. c. N. 5.
18 Capello, l. c. N. 166.
19 Augustine, l. c. VIII, p. 446.
20 Wernz, VI N. 345.
21 Canon 730.
22 Canon 736.

of canons 1056 and 1234 remaining in force, it pertains to a provincial council or a convention of the bishops of a province to determine the charges to be paid in the entire ecclesiastical province for the various acts of voluntary jurisdiction, or for the execution of rescripts of the Apostolic See, or on the occasion of administration of the sacraments or sacramentals. But whatever decision is reached must first receive the approbation of the Holy See before it takes effect.''

Suppose then a certain amount is named by the proper authority. If a cleric should exact more than this sum, would he be guilty of simony? Some reply in the affirmative on the ground that there is no just title of extrinsic labor or support, and hence the excess demanded constitutes a recompense for sacred ministrations.[23] Others deny the presence of simony unless the minister acted from the wrong motive of receiving a temporal for a spiritual object.[24] Capello correctly holds that inasmuch as we are engaged upon *materia odiosa* in this question, this second opinion can safely be followed as far as the suspension is concerned. However, even if a priest in requiring a sum greater than that fixed by law should not have an intention formally simoniacal, nevertheless he would sin against obedience and justice.[25]

''*Scienter*'' indicates that any diminution of imputability whatsoever will excuse from the censure.[26] Moreover, it modifies not only ''*promoti fuerint*'' but also ''*ministraverint vel receperint.*''[27]

23 Schmalzgrueber Lib. V, Tit. 3, N. 100; Reiffenstuel, Lib. V, T. 3 N. 200; Ballerini-Palmieri, Opus Theol. Mor. N. 282.

24 Noldin, l. c. 11, 194 b; Lehmkuhl, Theologia Moralis, 1, N. 534.

25 Capello, l. c. N. 166.

26 Canon 2229.

27 Chelodi, l. c. N. 93; Capello, l. c. N. 166.

CHAPTER X

RECEPTION OF ORDERS FROM ONE UNDER CENSURE

In early church law many prohibitions are found against the reception of orders from one who lacked or had been deprived of the exercise of his order. For it was said that no one was able to give what he himself did not possess. In some cases so rigorous were these decrees that they seem to have declared invalid the ordinations so received. For instance, in the Third Lateran Council convoked by Alexander III in 1179 it was stated that the ordinations performed by certain heresiarchs were considered null (*irritas*).[1] However, these expressions are to be interpreted as signifying nullity in respect to the exercise of the power bestowed. The ordination was valid substantially, but the one thus unlawfully ordained could not licitly perform the various functions of his order. These nullifying words of course could find verification and the ordination would essentially be invalid if either the required form, or necessary matter, or due intention in the minister were wanting.[2]

The next important legislation in this matter was enacted by Pius IX. In his constitution "*Apostolicae Sedis*" he declared that "All who have presumed to receive an order from one *nominatim* denounced as excommunicated, suspended, or interdicted, or from a notorious heretic or schismatic, incurred *ipso facto* a suspension from the order received which was reserved to the Roman Pontiff. But he who in good faith is ordained by one of the above designated persons lacks the right to exercise the order so received until he obtains a dispensation."

---

1 C. 5, C. IX, q. 1.
2 Gasparri, l. c. p. 71.

The New Law is very similar to that of Pius IX. "Those who presume to receive orders from one excommunicated, suspended, or interdicted by a declaratory or condemnatory sentence, or from a notorious apostate, heretic, or schismatic, contract *ipso facto* a suspension *a divinis* reserved to the Apostolic See. Be he who in good faith is ordained by any of the above mentioned persons lacks the exercise of the order so received until he is dispensed."[3]

Commentators on the "*Apostolicae Sedis*" disputed as to whether or not those who received episcopal consecration from prelates *nominatim* excommunicated, etc., incurred the suspension or prohibition therein decreed. Some maintained their immunity from this punishment on the score that the constitution spoke of "*ordine suscepto,*" and it was doubtful whether the episcopacy was an order in the strict sense of the word. Another reason assigned was that bishops were not explicitly named. This reason was based on the principle of law that bishops, unless expressly mentioned, did not come within the provisions of penal law. The more common opinion, however, included bishops also.[4] With the promulgation of the New Code all doubt ceased. Bishops now are certainly subject to this law. For canon 950 expressly asserts that the words *ordinare, ordo, ordinatio, sacra ordinatio* comprehend episcopal consecration as well as the major and minor orders enumerated in canon 949. As to the other objection, viz., that bishops are not subject to *latae sententiae* penalties of suspension and interdict unless expressly designated, it is sufficient to note with Pennachi that this exemption refers to legitimate bishops who enjoy free exercise of jurisdiction.[5]

According to the former discipline, the prelate who ordained had to be *nominatim* excommunicated,

---

3 Canon 2372.
4 Gasparri, l. c. N. 785; Pennachi, l. c. 11, p. 409.
5 Pennachi, l. c. 11, p. 411.

suspended, or interdicted. Hence, as Gasparri noted, he would have had to be *vitandus.*[6] *Nominatim* also required that the person excommunicated be declared such through a sentence by the proper authorities. His name, surname, and other identifying circumstances were to be so specified that he could not be taken for any one else. Accordingly, if he were only *collegialiter* interdicted, or excommunicated in any other way than *nominatim,* the one ordained would escape the censure.[7]

The New Law does not use the word *nominatim.* However, its effect is practically the same. But it is not necessary that the prelate under excommunication, etc., be *vitandus.* He could be *toleratus* provided a declaratory or condemnatory sentence had taken place.

The Code has added "notorious apostate" to "notorious heretic and schismatic" of the "*Apostolicae Sedis.*" Apostate is defined as one who totally abandons the Christian faith.[8]

What *notorious* signifies can be gleaned from canon 2197 which distinguishes two kinds of notorious delinquencies. The first, notorious by notoriety of law, is that which results either from a sentence pronounced by a competent judge, which sentence has passed into a *res judicata,* or from a confession on the part of the culprit made according to the norm of canon 1750. The second, notorious by notoriety of fact, is had when the crime is publicly known and was committed under such circumstances that it cannot be concealed by any artifice nor excused by any interpretation of law. Hence, a person who was guilty of either of these two kinds of notorious crimes would rightly be called a notorious sinner.

It should be observed that the effects of suspension are separable. Wherefore, if the suspension were not one that forbade the conferring of orders, even

---

6 Gasparri, l. c. N. 786.
7 Gasparri, l. c.
8 Canon 1325.

though it had been accompanied by a declaratory or condemnatory sentence, it would not render the ordination illicit, nor, as a consequence, would the person ordained by such a suspended prelate incur the penalty.[9]

"*Ordines*" in this canon must be taken in the strict sense of orders validly bestowed. Accordingly, if one should presumptuously receive an invalid ordination, e. g., from an Anglican bishop, he would not contract the censure.[10]

One who would receive tonsure from an excommunicated, etc., prelate would not incur the punishment of this canon. For by virtue of canon 950 "order" comprehends first tonsure only when the nature of the matter or the context does not demand its exclusion. Now, in the present instance both the nature of the subject matter and the context exclude tonsure. For one who receives tonsure cannot incur a suspension since tonsure does not confer upon him any power of order. Moreover, the suspension in question is "*a divinis.*"[11]

In the Old Law the penalty was suspension from the order illicitly received only. Now the suspension is "*a divinis.*" This, as is evident, is a heavier punishment since it forbids every act of the power of order which a cleric has obtained either through sacred ordination or by way of privilege.[12]

Presumption is required. Accordingly, even crass ignorance will excuse.

The second part of the canon contains a privation and not a censure or vindictive punishment.[13] One who in good faith is ordained by an excommunicated prelate, etc., lacks the exercise of the order so received until he is dispensed. This section is taken substantially from the "*Apostolicae Sedis.*" Commentators

---

9 Gasparri, l. c. No. 786; Blat, De Rebus, p. 753.
10 Gasparri, l. c.
11 Capello, l. c. N. 167; Blat, l. c. p. 753; Chelodi, l. c. N. 95.
12 Canon 2279, par. 2, n. 2.
13 Chelodi, l. c. N. 95.

of this constitution disputed concerning the person from whom dispensation should be obtained. Pennachi, basing his opinion on Decretal Law, stated that if one through crass ignorance received orders from an excommunicated prelate, etc., dispensation must come from the Roman Pontiff. But if his ignorance were simple or inculpable, he could be dispensed by his own bishop.[14] Gasparri, on the other hand, maintained that although according to the first decretal cited (C. 1, X. 1, 13) the bishop could not dispense from this prohibition to exercise the order received, if the ignorance were crass, supine, or affected, nevertheless, since this exception, of which no mention was made in the second decretal quoted (C. 2, X. 1, 13), had not been embodied in the constitution "*Apostolicae Sedis,*" it had ceased, and the prohibition, no matter what kind of ignorance existed, could be remitted by the bishop.[15]

Chelodi and Capello have adopted Gasparri's view. For they declare without making any distinction that dispensation is to be given by the person's own bishop ("*donec ab episcopo suo dispensetur*").[16]

---

14 "Sane si ab eodem sacros ordines scienter quis receperit, quia indignum se fecit, executionem officii non habebit; ubi autem non scienter poterit (nisi crassa et supina fuerit ignorantia) discretus pontifex dispensare." C. 1, X de ordinatis ab episcopo qui renunciavit episcopatui, 1, 13. "Cum clericis qui ab excommunicato Episcopo ignoranter ordines receperunt per suos poterit Episcopos dispensari." C. 2, X. 1, 13.

15 Gasparri, l. c. N. 787.

16 Capello, l. c. N. 168; Chelodi, l. c. N. 95.

CHAPTER XI

ILLEGAL ORDINATIONS

Ordination Without the Proper Dimissorial Letters

The Church has always recognized the rights of bishops over their own subjects. This is especially true in regard to ordination. For in this way the sanctity of holy orders is more easily guarded and maintained inasmuch as less opportunity is afforded unworthy candidates to force or find their unholy way into the sanctuary. As early as 343 the Synod of Sardica forbade bishops to entice subjects of another province into their own diocese for the purpose of ordination.[1] Because it often happened that excommunicated, apostate, or irregular clerics, or other unworthy aspirants to orders, betook themselves to distant lands to obtain ordination, Clement IV strictly enjoined upon the Italian bishops not to presume to ordain any ultramontane cleric without special permission from himself, or from the bishop of the diocese in which the candidate was born, or in which he had a benefice. This permission was to be exhibited in the form of letters which should contain a reasonable cause why the bishop himself would or could not ordain. If any were ordained in violation of this decree they became *ipso facto* suspended without any hope of obtaining a dispensation from the Apostolic See. Those who ordained illegally in this manner should receive suitable penances.[2] Later Gregory X (A. D. 1274) declared a *latae sententiae* suspension of one year from the conferring of orders against those who presumed to ordain clerics of an

1 C. 1, D. 71.
2 C. 1, 6, 1, 9.

alien parish without due permission.[3] The Council of Trent also framed important legislation on this subject. The suspension of one year from the conferring of orders was confirmed and renewed.[4] Other legislation was contributed by succeeding pontiffs, particularly by Sixtus V,[5] Clement VIII,[6] and Innocent XII.[7] Pius IX in his constitution "*Sedis Apostolicae*" decreed a suspension of one year from the administration of orders reserved to the Holy See to be incurred *ipso facto* by those who ordained an alien subject even under the pretext of a benefice to be conferred immediately or already conferred, but not at all sufficient, without the dimissorial letters of his bishop.

Finally, the New Code states that those who in violation of canon 955 (which provides that each one should be ordained by his own bishop or with legitimate dimissorial letters from the same) ordain a subject not their own without dimissorial letters of the proper bishop incur *ipso facto* a suspension of one year from the conferring of orders reserved to the Apostolic See.[8]

In order to determine when this suspension is incurred it will be necessary to ascertain who are *episcopi proprii,* who may grant dimissorial letters, etc.

Episcopus Proprius

In the Old Discipline there were five ways by which a person became subject to a certain bishop for the purpose of ordination, viz., origin, domicile, benefice, *familiaritas,* and incardination.[9] The New

3 C. 2, 6, 1, 9.
4 Sess. 23, Cap. 8, De Ref.
5 Const. "Sanctum et Salutare" 5 Jan. 1589.
6 Const. "Romanum Pontificem" 28 Feb. 1596.
7 Const. "Speculatores" 4 Nov. 1694.
8 Canon 2373, par. 1.
9 Wernz, II Pars. 2, N. 28 III.

Law, as far as the ordination of seculars is concerned, takes into consideration only origin and domicile. The *episcopus proprius* in respect to the ordination of seculars is that bishop only in whose diocese the candidate has a domicile together with origin, or a simple domicile without origin; but in this second case the candidate must confirm his intention of remaining in the diocese permanently with an oath, unless there is question of promoting to orders a cleric who is already incardinated in the diocese by means of first tonsure, or of promoting an aspirant who is destined to the service of another diocese according to the norm of canon 969, par. 2, or of promoting a professed religious of whom mention is made in canon 964, par. 4.[10]

This canon embodies new legislation. Formerly origin alone without domicile sufficed to constitute a person subject to a bishop. According to Pennachi, a candidate for orders was subject to a certain bishop by reason of origin if at the time of his birth his parents had a domicile in the bishop's diocese.[11] This was the law promulgated by Innocent XII in his constitution "*Speculatores.*"

What origin signifies can be drawn from canon 90. The place of origin of a child (*filii*), even of a neophyte, is that in which when the child was born the father, or if the child were illegitimate, or posthumous, the mother, had a domicile, or, in defect of a domicile, a quasi-domicile. If there be question of a child of *vagi*, the place of origin is that of birth. The place of origin of a foundling is that where it was discovered.

Heretofore quasi-domicile did not enter into the matter of origin. A candidate for orders became subject to a bishop by virtue of origin if at the time of his birth his parents had a domicile in the bishop's diocese. If his parents did not have a domicile in the diocese (or only had a quasi-domicile) and the aspirant

10 Canon 956.
11 Pennachi, l. c. II, p. 366.

was born there *per accidens,* e. g., while his parents were engaged in some temporary business, the candidate's proper bishop was that one in whose diocese the father was born.[12]

It should be noted, too, that the place of origin of a child of *vagi* is now that of birth, whereas formerly it was that wherein the father was born.

If at the time of the candidate's birth his father was a *vagus* but his mother had a domicile of her own,[13] Vermeersch thinks that by analogy of law the *locus originis* would be that of the mother's domicile. For in this case the child was not strictly speaking the offspring of *vagi* inasmuch as there was only one *vagus,* the father. And if the place of origin of a posthumous child is that wherein the mother had a domicile at the time of its birth it would seem that in the present instance the mother's place of domicile would determine the *locus originis* of her son.[14]

Domicile is acquired by residence in some parish or quasi-parish, or at least in a diocese, vicariate apostolic, or prefecture apostolic. Moreover, this residence either must be combined with the intention of remaining in the place perpetually unless some reason should necessitate a departure, or at least it must last for ten years.[15]

The conditions required in order to obtain a domicile for the purpose of ordination are much easier now than in the Old Discipline. From the constitution "*Speculatores*" of Innocent XII we learn what these conditions previously were. The candidate had to establish himself permanently in the place in such wise that either by residing there at least for ten years or by transferring to it the greater part of his goods and remaining therein for some time (three years)[16] he sufficiently demonstrated his purpose of

---

12 Pennachi, l. c. II, p. 366.
13 Canon 93, par. 1.
14 Vermeersch, l. c. I, N. 166.
15 Canon 92.
16 Wernz, II, Pars. 1, N. 28 III.

staying permanently. In either case he had to affirm under oath the sincerity of his intention.

Wernz deprecated the severity of these conditions. He thought that the period of ten years should be reduced to one; also that the transferrence of goods should not be demanded.[17] The Code has gone even further. Only a simple domicile is now required. Not even a stay of three years is necessary. Hence a candidate, if he has not already been incardinated in some place by tonsure, by merely entering a diocese and forming an intention to remain there permanently unless some reason necessitates his departure, and making the requisite oath, becomes subject to the bishop of that diocese. One exception would be the case of minors. Minors necessarily retain the domicile of those to whom they are subject.[18] Accordingly, they cannot obtain a domicile independently of their parents. Only in the event of their father, or mother, or others to whom they are subject, as the case may be, acquiring a domicile in a certain diocese can they also obtain a domicile there with a view to ordination.

Intention is no longer an essential element in the event of a person actually spending ten years in a place. Furthermore, the Code now allows the acquisition of a diocesan domicile.[19] Wherefore, by mere residence for ten years in a certain diocese, although in that time the person lived in many different parishes and formed no intention of continuing indefinitely or permanently in the diocese, a diocesan domicile would be acquired and would suffice together with the oath to obtain an *episcopus proprius*.

Domicile alone without the oath is sufficient in the case of one already incardinated in a diocese by means of first tonsure. The reason of this lies in the conditions laid down to obtain legitimately first tonsure. These conditions are the same as those

17 Wernz, II, Pars. 1, N. 28 III, footnote 44.
18 Canon 93.
19 Canon 92.

prescribed for major and minor orders in canon 956. For according to canon 950 "*ordinatio*" includes also first tonsure unless the nature of the matter or the context demands a different interpretation. Hence in order to receive tonsure lawfully, or to be legitimately incardinated in a certain diocese, one must have either his place of origin together with a domicile there or a simple domicile alone, but in this latter contingency he would have to make the required oath.[20]

Domicile alone without the oath also suffices when there is question of promoting an aspirant who is destined for the service of another diocese in accordance with canon 969, par. 2, or of promoting a professed religious, i. e., a religious whose ordination is governed by the law of seculars as stipulated in canon 964, par. 4. A distinction is drawn between ordaining a candidate destined for the service of another diocese (*qui servitio alius diocesis destinetur*)[21] and ordaining a candidate for another diocese (*pro cujus servitio promotus fuit*).[22] In the first case by virtue of canon 969, par. 2, ordination involves incardination in the diocese of the *Episcopus Proprius*. In the second case, however, according to canon 111, par. 2, the person ordained becomes incardinated, not in the diocese of the *Episcopus Proprius*, but in that for the service of which he was ordained.[23] As is quite evident, although not explicitly stated, simple domicile alone is sufficient also in this second instance.

In the matter of ordination vicars and prefects apostolic as well as abbots or prelates *nullius*, if they are endowed with the episcopal character, are made equal to a diocesan bishop. Even though they lack the episcopal character, nevertheless they can, within their own territory, but only during the duration of

---

20 Vermeersch, l. c. II, N. 239.

21 Canon 969, par. 2.

22 Canon 111, par. 2.

23 Response of the Pontifical Commission for the Authentic Interpretation of the Canons of the Code; 3 Aug. 1919. Monitore eccles. Ser. IV, vol. II, 57, which is quoted by Blat, De Rebus, p. 368.

their office, confer first tonsure and minor orders both to their own secular subjects according to the norm of canon 956 and also to others who exhibit legitimate dimissorial letters.[24]

This is new legislation. Formerly the *Episcopus vicinior* was the *episcopus proprius* of the secular and regular subjects of a prelate *nullius.*[25] Vicars and Prefects Apostolic had no right to ordain their subjects. Whenever they did so it was by virtue of a privilege granted by the Apostolic See.

It might be inquired, which bishop has the right to ordain a person who, having given up his domicile in a certain place, pursues his studies in another diocese for the service of some third diocese? This question could find application in the case of seminaries for the foreign missions. The Code makes no provision for such a person. His *episcopus proprius* is not the *episcopus originis,* since he has renounced the domicile of his place of origin. Nor is it the bishop of his residence or quasi-domicile, because he neither has a domicile there nor can he acquire one, and moreover he is unable to furnish the requisite oath of perpetual service. And finally it is not the bishop of the diocese to which he will eventually go, for he has not yet obtained a domicile in that place. Wherefore, until an authentic interpretation solves the difficulty recourse must be had to an apostolic indult.[26]

In regard to the ordination of religious, a governing abbot of regulars, even though he be not an abbot *nullius,* can confer first tonsure and minor orders provided the candidate is his subject by virtue of at least simple profession, and he himself is a priest and has legitimately received the abbatial blessing.[27]

The abbot must be an *abbas regiminis.* Hence, a titular abbot, or a commendatory abbot, or one who

24 Canon 957.
25 Wernz, II, N. 28 IV footnote 57.
26 Vermeersch, l. c. II N. 240.
27 Canon 964, par. 1.

has entirely renounced his office, may neither validly nor licitly confer tonsure and minor orders.[28]

DIMISSORIAL LETTERS

It was the mind of the Fathers of the Council of Trent that bishops, if possible, should ordain their own subjects. But if sickness prevented this personal ordination they should send (*dimittant*) the candidates who had been examined and approved to another bishop.[29] Permission thus given to another to ordain one's subjects may be imparted orally, but as a rule it is committed to writing. In either case it must be express.[30]

This permission is designated by the term *dimissorial letters.* According to Wernz, "Dimissoriae dicuntur litterae quibus proprius ordinandi Prelatus vi suae jurisdictionis rogat vel deputat episcopum sive specialiter vel generaliter determinatum, ut subdito suo, de cujus idoneitate simul authenticum dat testimonium, ordines conferat."[31]

The following can grant dimissorial letters for seculars as long as they retain jurisdiction in their territory:

1. *Episcopus proprius,* even though not yet consecrated, after he has legitimately taken possession of his diocese according to the norm of canon 334, par. 3, that is, as soon as either he himself or his proxy has exhibited the Apostolic Letters to the diocesan chapter in the presence of the secretary of the chapter or the diocesan chancellor.

2. The Vicar General, provided he has received a special mandate from the bishop.

3. The Vicar Capitular with the consent of the Chapter after a year from the time the See became vacant. Within the first year of vacancy, however,

---

28 Wernz, II, N. 27 II b.

29 Sess. XXIII, cap. 3.

30 Sess. XIV, cap. 2, de ref. "Expresso consensu aut litteris dimissoriis."

31 Wernz, II, N. 29 II.

the Vicar Capitular may grant dimissorial letters to the *arctati,* that is, to those who have already received a benefice or are going to receive one, or who are required for some office which the needs of the diocese demand be filled without delay. It should be noted that the Vicar Capitular must obtain not merely the advice, but the consent of the Chapter.

4. Vicar and Prefect Apostolic, Abbot or Prelate *Nullius,* even though they are not bishops. They may grant these letters for major as well as minor orders.[32] Hence, although the above mentioned prelates, if they have not received episcopal consecration, can confer only tonsure and minor orders upon their subjects, yet they may grant dimissorial letters to them for all the orders, both major and minor.

The Vicar Capitular's power is further restricted in that he is forbidden to give dimissorial letters to those who were rejected by the Bishop whose place he has taken.[33] This prohibition, however, is not *ad validitatem.* And so, if the Vicar Capitular should issue letters to one previously refused, he would act illicitly, but his letters would be legitimate in the sense of the word employed in canon 962.[34]

It might happen that after receipt of the dimissorial letters ordination would be delayed long enough, according to the law, for the candidate to contract some canonical impediment. This time is three months for soldiers and six months for others.[35] In such an event the bishop shall exact new testimonial letters from the candidate's Ordinary before he proceeds to the ordination.[36] This of course supposes that the ordinand has remained for the required period in his own diocese. If, however, he had spent the time in the

32 Canon 958, par. 1.
33 Canon 958, par. 2.
34 Blat, l. c. III p. 372.
35 Canon 994, par. 3.
36 Canon 960, par. 2.

diocese of the ordaining bishop, the latter is himself obliged to secure directly the necessary information.[37]

While bishops only are mentioned in this canon nevertheless it is quite evident that all those who can confer orders, even should they be only simple priests, are included.[38] This is confirmed by canon 215 which declares that an abbot or prelate *nullius* also comes under the name of bishop, unless the nature of the matter or the context of the words demands otherwise.

Dimissorial letters may be sent by the *episcopus proprius*, even by a suburbicarian cardinal bishop, to any bishop in communion with the Apostolic See, with the exception of a bishop of a rite different from that of the ordinand.[39] Excepting the clause which concerns suburbicarian cardinal bishops, this is only a repetition of the Old Law. Heretofore, these cardinal bishops could grant dimissorial letters only to the cardinal vicar of Rome to ordain their own secular subjects outside their diocese.[40] "*Episcopus proprius*" means not only the *episcopus proprius* of canon 956, but also all those designated in canon 958 as being competent to issue dimissorial letters for seculars.[41]

Dimissorial letters can be limited or revoked by the grantor or his successor. Once issued, however, they do not lose their force by the death, or loss of office, or loss of right in any way, of the grantor.[42] Wherefore, should a bishop receive legitimate dimissorial letters from a vicar capitular in accordance with canon 958, his right to ordain would not be lost if before using the letters a bishop was appointed and took possession of the vacant See, unless this new

---

37 Canon 960, par. 3.
38 Blat, l. c. III p. 374.
39 Canon 961.
40 Wernz, II N. 29 III footnote 69.
41 Blat, l. c. p. 375.
42 Canon 963.

bishop expressly revoked the letters of his predecessor.[43]

Exempt religious may not be licitly ordained by any bishop without the dimissorial letters of their own major superior.[44] "Religious" in this canon does not include novices.[45] But it does include those who have taken vows in a religious congregation[46] if the privilege of exemption has been especially granted them.[47] By expressly designating *major superiors* the Code takes away any power that *local superiors* may have had before of giving these letters.

When there is question of those of their subjects who have taken the simple triennial vows which according to canon 574 must precede perpetual vows, major superiors may grant dimissorial letters only for first tonsure and minor orders.[48] In order to give these letters for major orders solemn, or at least simple, perpetual profession must first take place. Furthermore, all indults granted to superiors for giving dimissorial letters for major orders to those of their subjects professed *a votis temporariis* are now revoked.[49]

The ordination of the members of any other religious body (that is, non-exempt) is governed (with respect to the concession of dimissorial letters) by the law of seculars.[50] Hence, the members of a non-exempt religious body, whether they are temporarily or perpetually professed, may receive dimissorial letters only from their *episcopus* proprius in accordance with the provisions of canon 958.[51]

Religious superiors may not send their candidates for orders to any bishop at all. Dimissorial letters

---

43 Gasparri, l. c. N. 888.
44 Canon 964, par. 2.
45 Canon 488, par. 7.
46 Canon 488, par. 7.
47 Canon 618, par. 1.
48 Canon 964, N. 3.
49 Canon 964, N. 4.
50 Canon 964, N. 4.
51 Fanfani, l. c. N. 214.

must be directed to the bishop of the diocese in which the religious house of the ordinand is located.[52] However, in certain circumstances another bishop could lawfully receive these letters, viz., if the diocesan bishop has given permission; if he is of a different rite; if he is absent; if he does not intend to have an ordination at the next appointed time (the appointed times are the Ember Saturdays, the Saturday before Passion Sunday, and Holy Saturday); and finally, if the Episcopal See is vacant and the prelate temporarily ruling is not a bishop. Certificates of the existence of one of these cases must be obtained by the ordaining bishop from the episcopal court.[53]

Even if an absent bishop should secure another prelate to ordain in his place at the regular time, the religious superior could still use his privilege of selecting any other bishop. A bishop, however, would not be considered absent if he merely obtained a substitute for the ordination, but did not himself depart from the diocese.[54]

If during the vacancy of an Episcopal See an administrator was appointed who lacked the episcopal character, but had the power of conferring tonsure and minor orders, would a religious superior still be allowed to send his candidates for tonsure and minor orders to the bishop of his choice? It would seem so because canon 966 states explicitly "*cum dioecesis vacet nec eam regat qui charactere episcopali polleat.*" Despite this, Vermeersch is of the opinion (*ni fallimur*) that in such circumstances the superior must have recourse to the administrator.[55]

Penalty: If a bishop or any of the other prelates above mentioned ordain the subject of another prelate without the proper dimissorial letters he suffers an *ipso facto* suspension of one year from the conferring

52 Canon 965.
53 Canon 966.
54 Gasparri, l. c. N. 922.
55 Vermeersch, l. c. N. 241, 5.

of orders, which suspension is reserved to the Holy See. It should be noted that the suspension is only from the conferring of orders. Hence the suspended prelate may legitimately exercise all his other episcopal functions or powers. This punishment is to last for a year unless before that time the Holy See grants a dispensation. At the expiration of a year it expires automatically.[56] The penalty would be incurred by one who conferred only first tonsure on another's subject without the requisite dimissorial letters. For "*ordinaverint*" comprehends also first tonsure.[57]

Ordination Without the Requisite Testimonial Letters

In order to prevent more surely the reception of unworthy candidates into the sacred ministry the Church requires her prelates to obtain evidence of the fitness of an aspirant who by residing outside his diocese for a certain length of time may have contracted a canonical impediment. This evidence is given in the form of testimonial letters.

Innocent XII in his constitution "*Speculatores*" ordered these letters to be secured by the *episcopus originis* from the Ordinary of the place in which candidates for first tonsure or orders had been born *ex accidenti* and had lived long enough to contract an impediment.[58] But the scope of this decree was too limited. It failed to provide for the case in which an aspirant stayed in a place in which he was not born *ex accidenti.* Hence, some canonists concluded that in such a contingency it was not necessary to demand testimonial letters. Their opinion was corroborated by a decree of the Sacred Congregation of the Council.[59] Notwithstanding this, the more common

56 Pennachi, l. c. II, p. 374.
57 Canon 950.
58 4 Nov. 1694.
59 17 March, 1708.

opinion upheld the necessity of the letters under these circumstances, and this view was supported by several later decisions of the Sacred Congregation of the Council.[60]

All doubts disappeared on the promulgation of the constitution "*Apostolicae Sedis*" of Pius IX. For in this constitution an *ipso facto* suspension of one year from the conferring of orders, which was reserved to the Apostolic See, was decreed against a bishop who ordained "subditum proprium qui alibi tanto tempore moratus sit, ut canonicum impedimentum contrahere ibi potuerit, absque Ordinarii loci litteris testimonialibus."

The Code repeats this suspension,[61] and also explicitly states the juridical time during which an impediment could be contracted. This time is for soldiers three months and for all others six months after puberty. But the ordaining bishop, if his prudence so dictates, may demand the testimonial letters even for a shorter stay, and also for the time before the age of puberty.

But if the local Ordinary either personally or through the agency of others has not acquired sufficient knowledge of the conduct of the candidate during the time he resided in his territory to enable him to affirm that no canonical impediment was contracted, or if the candidate has lived in so many dioceses that it is impossible or extremely difficult to demand testimonial letters from all the ordinaries of these places, the Ordinary shall oblige the aspirant to make the supplementary oath.

If after the receipt of these testimonial letters the ordination does not take place immediately, and the candidate again spends sufficient time in the same territory to incur an impediment, new testimonial letters of the local Ordinary are necessary.[62]

---

60 7 Feb. 1733; 14 Nov. 1733; 19 Aug. 1797.
61 Canon 2373, N. 2.
62 Canon 994.

Formerly some canonists required these testimonial letters even for those who, after the age of seven, but before the time of puberty, had lived for the stated period in a strange diocese.[63] For, they said, while it is true that such are not able to incur censures or irregularities *ex delicto,* yet their moral life during that time may be of such a nature as to render them unfit candidates for holy orders. Others placed puberty as the time after which consideration could be given to the six or three months' residence in alien territory.[64] The Code has decided in favor of the latter opinion.

A decree of the Sacred Congregation of the Council ordered testimonial letters to be obtained "*pro clericis ordinandis jam militiae addictis*" from the ordinaries in whose dioceses they had spent at least three months.[65] This of course referred only to cleric soldiers. The New Law makes no distinction. All soldiers, whether cleric or lay, need testimonial letters from the ordinaries in whose territory they have tarried at least three months.

In the old discipline before a bishop could resort to the supplementary oath he first had to have recourse to the Holy See.[66] Since the Code makes no mention of this recourse, it is no longer necessary.[67]

A bishop would not incur the suspension if he failed to secure the testimonial letters for a shorter residence than six or three months, as the case might be, or for the period preceding puberty, even if special circumstances might render them necessary. The reason of this is because the bishop is only obliged by the law to act if the stay has actually lasted six or three months. For a less time than the stipulated period he may *pro sua prudentia* demand the letters,

---

63 Gasparri, l. c. N. 731.
64 Wernz, II N. 29 V e.
65 Coll. Prop. de Prop. Fide, N. 1886.
66 Wernz, II N. 29 V e.
67 Capello, l. c. N. 170 footnote 4.

but if he should not do so he would not violate the law.[68]

Would a bishop who neglected to obtain the requisite testimonials contract the penalty if he did not himself ordain the candidate but gave dimissorial letters to another prelate for the ordination? An affirmative answer seems necessary if we regard only the end or purpose of the law. But since in this matter we are treating *de odiosis* and the law expressly states *"qui subditum proprium . . . . ordinaverit"* probably the suspension is not incurred.[69] In regard to the *episcopus alienus* who ordains in such a case, the penalty is not incurred even if he should know with certainty that the testimonial letters had not been secured. The reason again is because the law explicitly punishes only those who ordain their own subjects.[70]

These letters are to be granted by the *Ordinarii locorum.* Hence all those designated in canon 198 as *Ordinarii locorum* may issue these testimonials. In the Old Law Gasparri held that the vicar general without a special mandate could not give the letters.[71] Wernz, on the other hand, maintained his right to do so even without the mandate.[72] Inasmuch as the vicar general by virtue of canon 198 is an *Ordinarius loci,* his right is now clear and certain.

Ordination Without a Canonical Title

Since it would be gravely irreverent to permit those enrolled in the holy ministry to be compelled to beg or adopt other unbecoming methods to secure a livelihood, with consequent dishonor to their sacred order, the Church from her earliest years has insisted on the need of a canonical title for candidates to

68 Capello, l. c. N. 170.
69 Capello, l. c.
70 Capello, l. c. N. 170.
71 Gasparri, l. c. N. 710.
72 Wernz, II N. 29 V e.

orders. This title may be defined as a security given to a clergyman to insure his honorable maintenance, thereby enabling him to be promoted to higher orders.[73]

The Council of Chalcedon (A. D. 451) permitted sacred orders to be conferred only on those aspirants who by taking up a certain office in the Church had made provision for their decent living and support. So rigorously was this decree insisted upon that ordinations performed without the necessary title were declared null and void.[74] This nullity, however, meant only that the person thus ordained was forbidden to exercise his orders.[75]

Only two titles were at first recognized, benefice and religious profession. To these Alexander III in the Third Council of the Lateran (A. D. 1178) added that of patrimony. Moreover, he required the title only for deaconship and priesthood. Later Innocent III (1198) extended this requirement to the orders *infra diaconatum.* In practice, however, it was never demanded for orders lower than sub-deaconship. The Council of Trent also enacted legislation to correct abuses in this matter.[76] Several popes afterwards made further contributions to the laws already existing. Among these were Pius V in his constitution "*Romanus Pontifex,*"[77] Urban VIII in his constitution "*Ad uberes,*"[78] and Pius IX in his "*Apostolicae Sedis.*"[79]

In the old legislation no suspension was incurred by a bishop who simply ordained a candidate to orders without a canonical title. Alexander III had imposed upon bishops who thus ordained merely an obligation to furnish the cleric with the necessities of life.[80]

73 Augustine, l. c. IV P. 465.
74 C. 2, Dist. 70.
75 Wernz, II N. 91.
76 Sess. XXI cap. 2 de ref; and Sess. XXIII c. 16 de ref.
77 Oct. 14, 1568.
78 May 18, 1638.
79 Oct. 12, 1869.
80 C. 4, X de praeb. III 5.

But a suspension of three years from the conferring of orders was incurred if, in addition to ordaining without a title, the bishop had made a compact with the aspirant in which the latter promised not to seek support afterwards from the former. Furthermore, the one thus ordained was *ipso facto* suspended from the execution of his orders until dispensation was obtained from the Apostolic See.[81]

Pius IX in his "Apostolicae Sedis" declared "Suspensionem per triennium a collatione ordinum ipso jure incurrunt aliquem ordinantes absque titulo beneficii vel patrimonii cum pacto ut ordinatus non petat ab ipsis alimenta." Since this law failed to make any mention of support to be provided by the bishop Pennachi concluded that the obligation was no longer binding. He also asserted the necessity of the presence of an agreement between the bishop and the ordinand concerning support in order that the penalty might be contracted.[82]

According to the New Law the presence of a pact is not necessary. Canon 2373 states that an *ipso facto* suspension of one year from the conferring of orders, which is reserved to the Apostolic See, is incurred by those who promote any one to major orders without a canonical title. If, however, an agreement had been entered into with reference to non-support, it would be absolutely void.[83] And if any prelates, without an apostolic indult, knowingly ordain or permit to be ordained their subjects in sacred orders without a canonical title, they and their successors must furnish the necessities of life to these clerics, if they are in need, until such time as provision is otherwise made for their means of sustenance.[84] Note that the obligation of furnishing support only binds in case the

81 C. 45, X de Simonia.
82 Pennachi, l. c. II p. 357.
83 Canon 980, par. 3.
84 Canon 980, par. 2.

cleric is actually in need (*"eidem egenti alimenta necessaria praebere"*).

The titles for secular clerics are benefice, and, if that is lacking, either patrimony or pension.[85] Benefice, therefore, is regarded as the principal title. These titles must be really secure for the entire life of the persons ordained, and also truly sufficient to provide them with a suitable livelihood in accordance with the norms laid down by the Ordinaries for different circumstances of times and places.[86]

If none of the three titles cited above is available, the title *servitium dioecesis* may be substituted, or, in places subject to the Sacred Congregation of the Propagation of the Faith, the title *missio.* But if these titles are employed, the ordinand must under oath declare that he will devote himself perpetually to the service of the diocese or mission under the authority of the *pro tempore* local Ordinary.[87]

For regulars the canonical title is solemn religious profession, or, as it is called, title of poverty. For religious of simple perpetual vows, the title is *mensa communis,* congregation, or another similar one according to the norm of the constitutions.

All other religious, as far as the canonical title is concerned, are governed by the law of seculars.[88]

Would a prelate incur the suspension if he ordained a candidate whose title, while real, was insufficient to afford him a decent living? In the old discipline Pennachi thought that since the constitution of Pius IX read *"sine titulo"* without any qualification as to sufficiency or insufficiency, the bishop escaped the penalty in such a case.[89] Capello draws a distinction. "If the bishop knows with certainty the title's insufficiency, he incurs the suspension, because, according to canon 979, par. 2, a title certainly

85 Canon 979, par. 1.
86 Canon 979, par. 2.
87 Canon 981.
88 Canon 982.
89 Pennachi, l. c. II p. 364.

inadequate to yield the cleric a suitable sustenance is not a canonical title, and hence, if a candidate is ordained with the same, he is to be regarded as ordained without a title. But if the bishop is not aware of the title's inadequacy, the penalty is not contracted.'[90] A further distinction, however, must be made. Canon 2373 does not employ "*praesumpserit*" or other similar word. Wherefore, according to canon 2229, par. 3, n. 2, if the ignorance were due to carelessness that was gravely culpable, it would not excuse from the penalty. But if the carelessness or remissness were not gravely culpable, since then no serious sin would have been committed, the penalty would not be incurred.

The suspension affects only the *episcopus proprius* and not the one who ordains another's subject with the proper dimissorial letters.[91]

Illegal Ordination of a Religious

According to canon 966, as was noted previously in treating of dimissorial letters, a religious superior may lawfully send dimissorial letters to the bishop of another diocese than that in which the religious house is located only in the following cases: When the diocesan bishop has given permission; when he is of a different rite; when he is absent from his diocese; when he does not intend to hold an ordination at the next period designated by canon law; or, finally, when the Episcopal See is vacant and there is no prelate ruling *pro tempore* who has the episcopal character.

Moreover, it is necessary that in each individual case authentic evidence of the presence of one of the above mentioned conditions be obtained by the ordaining bishop from the episcopal court of the diocese in which the house of the religious is situated.

90 Capello, l. c. N. 171.
91 Chelodi, l. c. N. 94; Pennachi, l. c. p. 361.

If a bishop should ordain a religious in violation of this law he would incur an *ipso facto* suspension of one year from the conferring of orders, which is reserved to the Apostolic See. An exception, however, is made in regard to those religious who have the privilege of choosing any bishop they desire for ordination.[92] For example, Gregory XIII in his constitution "*Pium et utile*" granted to certain religious superiors the faculty of sending dimissorial letters "*ad quemcunque Episcopum habentem gratiam et communionem cum Sede Apostolica.*"[93] Any bishop, of course, may ordain such religious without infringing the provisions of canon 966.

Even if an authentic document had not been procured from the episcopal court, as stipulated in canon 966, par. 2, Capello is of the opinion that a bishop would not suffer the suspension provided he were certain from other reliable sources that one of the required conditions actually existed.[94]

---

92 Canon 2373, N. 4.
93 22 Sept. 1582.
94 Capello, l. c. N. 172.

CHAPTER XII

ILLEGAL RECEPTION OF ORDERS

In the preceding canon a penalty is decreed only against those who illicitly ordain. Now in canon 2374 the Code provides punishments also for persons unlawfully promoted to orders. Those who without dimissorial letters, or with false dimissorial letters, or before they have attained the canonical age, or *per saltum* wilfully receive orders are *ipso facto* suspended from the order received. Also, those who are ordained without testimonial letters, or who take orders while subject to a censure, irregularity, or other impediment, should be afflicted with severe punishments according to the circumstances of the case.

Dimissorial letters are regarded as false if they are forged *in toto*, or if their original contents have been materially altered. In the latter contingency it is necessary that the sense be changed in some substantial part of the document. Otherwise, the suspension would not be incurred.[1] Letters used after due revocation also would be considered false.[2]

The canonical age for sub-deaconship is the twenty-first completed year, for deaconship, the twenty-second completed year, and for priesthood, the twenty-fourth completed year.[3] This is the same as in the old discipline. In respect to tonsure and minor orders no age is specifically determined. Nevertheless, a certain limit exists. No one, whether secular or religious, may be promoted to first tonsure until he has commenced his theological course.[4] By theological

1 Capello, l. c. N. 179.
2 Cerato, l. c. N. 119.
3 Canon 975.
4 Canon 976, par. 1.

course is meant theology in the strict sense. Nothing is said in reference to minor orders. But of course they may not be conferred until one has first received tonsure. Hence, as can readily be seen, a mature age is now implicitly required for both the reception of tonsure and minor orders. Formerly common law demanded only the completion of the seventh year for these orders, although by particular statute a higher age was sometimes designated.[5]

In Decretal Law one who, in bad faith, was ordained *in sacris* before the canonical age suffered a *ferendae sententiae* suspension from the use of the order illegitimately received until he attained the legal age.[6] Later Pius II in his constitution "*Cum ex sacrorum*" declared such a person suspended *ipso facto* from all sacred orders, i. e., both from those rightly received and from those unlawfully received, without any limitation of time.[7] Pius IX in his "*Apostolicae Sedis*" made no mention of this censure, and hence it was automatically abrogated. Gasparri notes, however, that while no suspension bound a cleric thus illegally ordained, yet he could not solemnly perform the functions of the order without a dispensation until the stipulated age was attained. This was due to the fact that the law which prohibited the reception of an order previously to a certain age also forbade the exercise of the same order before that age, if by some means it were prematurely received.[8]

According to the New Code, one who wilfully receives an order before he has attained the required age incurs an unreserved *ipso facto* suspension from the order received. Inasmuch as this suspension is a censure and not reserved, any confessor may absolve from it *in foro sacramentali*.[9] Moreover, if absolution is imparted in the internal forum the delinquent may,

---

5 Gasparri, l. c. N. 487, 488, 489.
6 C. 14, X de temporibus ordinationum 1, 11.
7 17 Nov. 1461.
8 Gasparri, l. c. N. 494.
9 Canon 2253, par. 1.

remoto scandalo, hold himself absolved in respect to the external court.[10] Hence, if the culprit alone knew of his offence, or if it were known only to a few who would not divulge it, he could lawfully exercise the functions of his order after obtaining absolution in the sacramental forum. No further absolution in the external court would be necessary. But should the *delictum* come to the knowledge of his superior, the latter could urge the continuance of the suspension until absolution had been given in the external forum, unless the fact of sacramental absolution were proved, or at least legitimately presumed in the external court.[11]

Ordinations *per saltum* have been prohibited from the earliest years of the Church. Both the Council of Nice in 325 (canon 2) and that of Sardica in 343 (canon 10) prescribed the gradual conferring of orders. In order that the prohibitions against *per saltum* ordinations might become effective suitable sanctions had to be enacted. Alexander II in 1065 ordained a suspension from the orders received *per saltum.*[12] The Council of Trent indirectly approved this penalty by giving bishops the power of granting a dispensation to those promoted *per saltum, si non ministraverint.*[13] It was necessary, however, before a cleric could solemnly exercise the order to which he had been *per saltum* advanced that he should first receive the order omitted.[14] Pius IX did not list this suspension, which, according to Wernz, was undoubtedly *latae sententiae,*[15] among the censures compiled in his "*Apostolicae Sedis.*" Furthermore, it was not directly decreed by the Council of Trent. Accordingly, it now ceased to exist. But the prohibition to solemnly

---

10 Canon 2251.
11 Canon 2251.
12 C. 1, D. 52.
13 Sess. XXIII, Chap. XIV.
14 Gasparri, l. c. N. 498.
15 Wernz, II, N. 72.

administer the order received *per saltum* until reception of the order passed over still remained.[16]

The New Code simply declares that orders should be conferred *gradatim* in such wise that ordinations *per saltum* are absolutely forbidden.[17] A wilful violation of this canon entails an *ipso facto* unreserved suspension from the order illegitimately received. Full knowledge and deliberation must accompany the act. Grave fear would excuse from the penalty.[18] Capello observes that while there is no question of a reserved suspension, nevertheless absolution from the censure would not permit the cleric immediately to exercise the order illegally obtained. The order pretermitted must first be conferred.[19]

The word "orders" in this canon does not include first tonsure. For although dimissorial letters of the *episcopus proprius* are needed for a candidate for tonsure, nevertheless tonsure confers no spiritual power from which its recipient could suffer a suspension.[20]

The suspension is from the order received only and not from any other orders previously obtained.

Innocent XII in his constitution "*Speculatores*" decreed an *ipso facto* suspension from the orders received against clerics ordained without the necessary testimonial letters. This penalty was abrogated on the promulgation of the "*Apostolicae Sedis.*" The Code now ordains a *ferendae sententiae* punishment to be determined according to circumstances for this offence.

In early Church law reception of orders by one burdened with an irregularity resulted in ejection of the offender from the clerical state.[21] This penalty was later mitigated. Before the New Law if one

---

16 Gasparri, l. c. N. 498.
17 Canon 977.
18 Canon 2229.
19 Capello, l. c. N. 179.
20 Capello, l. c.
21 Council of Nice, Canons 9 and 10.

knowingly received orders while subject to an irregularity, besides being forbidden to exercise the orders received, he was also to be punished according to the prudence of his ecclesiastical superiors.[22]

The New Code decrees that if one subject to an irregularity presumptuously takes orders he should suffer a punishment in accordance with the circumstances of the case.

---

22 Wernz, II, N. 103, footnote 53.

CHAPTER XIII

MIXED MARRIAGES WITHOUT A DISPENSATION

Mixed marriages, owing to their harmful consequences, find no favor in the eyes of the Church. Pastors are instructed to deter as far as possible the faithful from entering into such dangerous unions. Should a Catholic contract, or rather, attempt marriage with a non-Catholic before a non-Catholic minister in his religious capacity, he incurs *ipso facto* an excommunication reserved to the Ordinary.[1]

Another penalty for mixed marriages is enacted in canon 2375. Catholics who dare to enter into a mixed marriage, even though valid, without a dispensation of the Church are *ipso facto* excluded from the legitimate ecclesiastical acts and the sacramentals until they have obtained a dispensation from the Ordinary.

Chelodi refers this punishment not only to marriages between Catholics and baptized non-Catholics, but also to those between Catholics and Infidels.[2] Blat[3] and Sole,[4] on the other hand, restrict it to the former class, i. e., to those unions contracted with the impediment of mixed religion from which no dispensation has been secured. The opinion of the latter would appear to be the correct one. For the canon imposing this penalty is contained in the title which treats of crimes committed in the administration and reception of the sacraments. Now there can be no question of the reception of the sacrament of matrimony between a Catholic and an Infidel without

1 Canon 2319.
2 Chelodi, l. c. N. 96.
3 Blat, l. c. p. 756.
4 Sole, l. c. N. 436.

the requisite dispensation. Furthermore, it is commonly maintained that even if a dispensation is obtained, a Catholic who marries an Infidel does not receive the sacrament. Chelodi himself subscribes to this opinion.[5] Hence, the penalty seems applicable only to the case in which a Catholic contracts marriage with a baptized non-Catholic in accordance with the form prescribed by the Code, but without having first obtained a dispensation from the impediment of mixed religion. This might happen if the non-Catholic party pretended to be a Catholic and the pastor of the Catholic party failed to make due inquiries.

"*Ausi fuerint*" signifies complete imputability. Accordingly, if the Catholic party were deceived by the Protestant, the punishment would not be incurred.

The ecclesiastical acts are as follows: The office of administrator of ecclesiastical goods; the functions of judge, *auditor, relator, defensor vinculi, promotor justitiae et fidei,* notary, chancellor, *cursor, apparitor,* lawyer and procurator in ecclesiastical cases, sponsors in the sacraments of baptism and confirmation, voting in ecclesiastical elections, exercising the *jus patronatus.*[6] Some of these functions, as is evident, do not apply to lay persons.

Blat observes that exclusion from the sacramentals means those sacramentals which consist of actions and not those which are things (*res*), e. g., holy water.[7]

The penalty is a vindictive one and lasts until dispensation is granted by the Ordinary.

---

5 Chelodi, Jus Matrimoniale, N. 6.
6 Canon 2256.
7 Blat, l. c. p. 756.

BIBLIOGRAPHY

SOURCES

Acta Apostolicae Sedis, Romae, 1909-1921.
Acta Sanctae Sedis, Romae, 1865-1908.
Bullarium Bened. P. XIV, Mechliniae, 1826.
Bullarium Romanum, Aug. Taurin, 1846-1872.
Canones et Decreta Concilii Tridentini, Romae, 1904.
Canonical Legislation Concerning Religious, Authorized English Translation, Rome, 1918.
Codex Juris Canonici, Romae, 1917.
Collectanea S. Cong. de Prop. Fide (1622-1906), Romae, 1907.
Corpus Juris Canonici (Richter) Lipsiae, 1839.
Hefele, History of the Councils of the Church, Edinburgh, 1895.
Mansi, Amplissima Coll. Concil. Parisiis, 1901-1913.
Rituale Romanum, Taurini, 1917.

AUTHORS

Alphonsus St. Theologia Moralis, Ratisbonae, 1846.
Augustine, A Commentary on the New Code of Canon Law, 8 volumes, St. Louis, 1922.
Ayrinhac, Penal Legislation in the New Code of Canon Law, New York, 1920.
Ballerini-Palmieri, Opus Theol. Moral. Prati, 1890.
Birkhaeuser, History of the Church, Rome, 1888.
Blat, De Rebus, Romae, 1920.
Blat, De Personis, Romae, 1921.
Bucceroni, Commentarius in Const. Bened. XIV "Sac. Poenitentiae," Lovanii, 1884.
Capello, De Censuris, Aug. Taurin, 1919.
Capello, De Sacramentis, Vol. I, Aug. Taurin, 1921.
Catholic Encyclopedia, 15 volumes, New York, 1917.

Cavigioli, De Censuris Latae Sententiae, Torino, 1918.
Cerato, Censurae Vigentes Ipso Facto, Patavii, 1918.
Chelodi, Jus Poenale, Tridenti, 1920.
Chelodi, Jus Matrimoniale, Tridenti, 1921.
Cocchi, Normae Generales, Aug. Taurin, 1921.
Cocchi, De Personis, Aug. Taurin, 1922.
D'Annibale, Commentarium in Const. "Apost. Sedis," Prati, 1894.
D'Annibale, Summa Theologiae Moralis, Romae, 1892.
Fanfani, De Jure Religiosorum, Romae, 1920.
Farrugia, Commentarium in Censuris Latae Sententiae, Melitae, 1921.
Ferreris, Compendium Theol. Moral. Barcelona, 1919.
Gasparri, De Sacra Ordinatione, Parisiis, 1893.
Gasparri, De Eucharistia, Parisiis, 1897.
Genicot, Institutiones Theol. Moral. Bruxellis, 1921.
Gennari, Quistioni Teologico Morali, Romae, 1907.
Gury-Ballerini, Compendium Theologiae Moralis, Romae, 1887.
Hickey, Irregularities and Simple Impediments in the New Code of Canon Law, Washington, 1920.
Irish Ecclesiastical Record, Vol. XII, July to Dec. 1918, Vol. XIV, July to Dec. 1919, Dublin.
Irish Theological Quarterly, January, 1918, Dublin.
Lega, De Delictis et Poenis, Romae, 1902.
Lehmkuhl, Theologia Moralis, Friburgi, 1914.
Marchant, Hortus Pastorum, Coloniae Agrippinae, 1699.
Maroto, Institutiones Juris Canonicae, Romae, 1919.
Motry, Diocesan Faculties according to the Code of Canon Law, Washington, 1922.
Noldin, Theologia Moralis, Oeniponte, 1920.
Ojetti, Synopsis Rerum Moralium et Juris Pontificii, Romae, 1914.
Pennachi, Commentarium in Const. "Apostolicae Sedis," Romae, 1883.
Petrovits, The New Church Law on Matrimony, Phila. 1921.

Planchard, De Const. Benedicti XIV "Sac. Poen." Engolismae, 1879.

Pruemmer, Brevis Conspectus Mutationum Theol. Moral., Friburgi, 1919.

Pruemmer, Manuale Moralis Theologiae, Friburgi, 1923.

Reiffenstuel, Jus Canonicum Universum, Venetiis, 1726.

Schmalzgrueber, Jus Ecclesiasticum Universum, Romae, 1845.

Sole, De Delictis et Poenis, Romae, 1920.

Vermeersch, Summa Novi Juris Canonici, Brugis, 1921.

Vermeersch, Epitome Juris Canonici, Brugis, 1922.

Vlaming, Praelectiones Juris Matrimonii, Bussum in Hollandia, 1919.

Wernz, Jus Decretalium, Prati, 1915.

Universitas Catholica Americae

Washingtonii, D. C.

Sacra Facultas Theologica

1922-1923

No. 17

CANONES

DEUS LUX MEA

CANONES

QUOS

AD DOCTORATUS GRADUM

IN

JURE CANONICO

Apud Universitatem Catholicam Americae

CONSEQUENDUM

PUBLICE PROPUGNABIT

GEORGIUS LAURENTIUS MURPHY

Sacerdos Archidioecesis Philadelphiensis

JURIS CANONICI LICENTIATUS

HORA IX A. M., DIE XXIX MAII, A. D. MCMXXIII

CANONES

I.	Canones	1-7	De Codicis ambitu.
II.	Canones	8-11	De legibus ecclesiasticis in genere.
III.	Canones	12-14	De legum ecclesiasticarum subiectis.
IV.	Canones	15-16	De legum effectibus.
V.	Canones	17-24	De legis interpretatione.
VI.	Canones	25-30	De consuetudine.
VII.	Canones	31-35	De temporis supputatione.
VIII.	Canones	36-62	De rescriptis.
IX.	Canones	63-79	De privilegiis.
X.	Canones	82-86	De dispensationibus.
XI.	Canones	87-89	De personis in genere.
XII.	Canones	90-95	De domicilio et quasi-domicilio.
XIII.	Canones	96-98	De consanguinitate et affinitate.
XIV.	Canones	108-110	De clericis in genere.
XV.	Canones	111-117	De clericorum incardinatione.
XVI.	Canones	120-614	De privilegio fori.
XVII.	Canon	145	De officii ecclesiastici notione.
XVIII.	Canones	196-210	De potestate ordinaria et delegata.
XIX.	Canones	215-217	De divisione dioecesarum.
XX.	Canones	518-523	De confessariis religiosorum.

XXI. Canones 745-754 De subiecto baptismi.

XXII. Canones 853-866 De subiecto Sacrae Communionis.

XXIII. Canones 893-900 De reservatione peccatorum.

XXIV. Canones 940-944 De subiecto extremae unctionis.

XXV. Canones 1012-1015 De matrimonio in genere.

XXVI. Canones 1043-1044 De impedimentis in periculo mortis.

XXVII. Canones 1060-1064 De impedimento mixtae religionis.

XXVIII. Canones 1133-1137 De convalidatione simplici.

XXIX. Canones 1138-1141 De sanatione in radice.

XXX. Canones 1142-1143 De secundis nuptiis.

XXXI. Canones 1552-1554 De iudicii ecclesiastici notione, objecto, et divisione.

XXXII. Canones 1594-1596 De tribunali secundae instantiae.

XXXIII. Canones 1636-1639 De loco et tempore iudicii.

XXXIV. Canones 1679-1683 De actione ob nullitatem actorum.

XXXV. Canones 1690-1692 De mutuis petitionibus.

XXXVI. Canones 1825-1828 De presumptionibus.

XXXVII. Canones 1960-1965 De foro competenti in causis matrimonialibus.

XXXVIII. Canones 1986-1989 De appellatione in causis matrimonialibus.

XXXIX.	Canones 1990-1992	De processu administrativo in causis matrimonialibus.
XL.	Canones 2186-2194	De suspensione ex informata conscientia.
XLI.	Canones 2195-2198	De notione delicti eiusque divisione.
XLII.	Canones 2209-2211	De complicibus in delicto.
XLIII.	Canones 2212-2214	De conatu delicti.
XLIV.	Canon 2229	De causis excusantibus a poenis.
XLV.	Canones 2236-2240	De poenarum remissione.
XLVI.	Canones 2241-2244	De censuris in genere.
XLVII.	Canones 2245-2247	De reservatione censurarum.
XLVIII.	Canones 2252-2254	De absolutione censurarum in periculo mortis et in urgenti casu.
XLIX.	Canones 2306-2311	De remediis poenalibus.
L.	Canon 2319	De haeresi faventibus.
LI.	Canon 2339	De sepultura ecclesiastica.
LII.	Canon 2350	De crimine abortus.
LIII.	Canon 2364	De delictis in administratione sacramentorum in genere.
LIV.	Canon 2365	De confirmatione.
LV.	Canon 2366	De iurisdictione.
LVI.	Canon 2367	De absolutione complicis.
LVII.	Canon 2368	De crimine sollicitationis.

LVIII.	Canon	2369	De violatione sigilli sacramentalis.
LIX.	Canones	2370-2374	De ordine.
LX.	Canon	2375	De mixta religione.

Vidit Sacra Facultas:

CAROLUS F. AIKEN, S. T. D., p. t. Decanus

H. SCHUMACHER, S. T. D., p. t. Secretis.

Vidit Rector Universitatis:

†THOMAS J. SHAHAN, S. T. D., J. U. L., LL. D.

BIOGRAPHY

George Lawrence Murphy was born May 1, 1891, in Philadelphia, Pa. He received his elementary education at St. Edward's Parochial School, and his secondary training at the Roman Catholic High School of the same city. In September, 1913, he entered St. Charles Seminary, Overbrook, Pa., and was ordained to the priesthood on May 21, 1921. The following September he entered the Catholic University of America, Washington, D. C., and attended the lectures of Monsignor Filippo Bernardini, Rev. Dr. Patrick J. Healy, and Rev. Dr. John A. Ryan, to all of whom he hereby expresses his sincere thanks.

www.ingramcontent.com/pod-product-compliance
Lightning Source LLC
LaVergne TN
LVHW050203080826
844660LV00012B/346

9780813222080